SLAVERY IN THE ISLAMIC MIDDLE EAST

SLAVERY IN THE ISLAMIC MIDDLE EAST

Shaun E. Marmon

EDITOR

Markus Wiener Publishers
Princeton

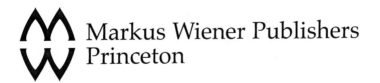

Third printing, 2014.

For information write to: Markus Wiener Publishers
231 Nassau Street, Princeton, NJ 08542
www.markuswiener.com

Library of Congress Cataloging-in-Publication Data

Slavery in the Islamic Middle East/Shaun Marmon, editor.
Includes bibliographical references.
ISBN-13: 978-1-55876-168-1 (hardcover : alk. paper)
ISBN-13: 978-1-55876-169-8 (paperback : alk. paper)
1. Slavery—Africa, North. 2. Slavery—Egypt—History—1250–1517. 3. Mamelukes—History. 4. Slavery and Islam-Africa, North. I. Marmon, Shaun Elizabeth.
HT1321.S557 1998
306.3'62'0961—dc21 97-40143
CIP

Markus Wiener Publishers books are printed in the United States of America on acid-free paper, and meet the guidelines for permanence and durability of the Committee on Production Guidelines for Book Longevity of the Council on Library Resources.

Contents

Introduction

SHAUN E. MARMON

The following articles are meant to serve as contributions to the ongoing study of slavery in Islamic societies. The perspectives and methodologies of the authors are, however, quite distinct. The focus ranges from transregional civilization to local community, from the medieval period to the nineteenth century. We see slaves in a variety of roles: as servants, as soldiers, as agricultural laborers, as concubines, as valued members of households, and as disposable property.

Islamic law provided a powerful and highly articulated paradigm for slavery, manumission, and clientage. This paradigm, however, is fraught with tensions and ambiguities. The slave is both person and property. The natural condition of human beings is freedom but enslavement is sanctioned by God as a punishment for unbelief. It is these very tensions, one might argue, that allows for the fluid status of the slave in many Muslim societies.

The relationship between the legal paradigm and social reality is one of the most important questions confronting anyone who undertakes the study of slavery in an Islamic context. There are times when slavery as constructed by Islamic law and slavery as practiced by Muslim communities seem to coincide with remarkable symmetry. But this symmetry cannot be taken for granted. Individuals and communities negotiated, interpreted, and at times blatantly violated the principles of the shariʿa.

David Ayalon, a pioneer in the field of Mamluk studies, devoted the greater part of his career to the study of military slavery. His writings on the subject have influenced almost every scholar working on the history of the medieval Middle East. While this volume was in preparation, David Ayalon died in Jerusalem at the age of eighty-four. Professor Ayalon's loss will be deeply felt by the international scholarly community. His legacy will live on in his many students and in his classic writings on the Mamluks. His contribution to this volume, however, is not so much about slavery as an institution as it is about the relationship between civilization and military power. The military slave serves as a starting point for a series of reflections on the comparison of civilizations that take us well into the modern period. Like all such big theories, Toynbee's and Huntington's included, Ayalon's forces us to look at big issues. But it is also open to debate. Does the category "civilization," whether it is Western Civilization or Islamic Civilization, allow for the diversity of individual societies and the nuances of historical change?

My article addresses the representations of slavery, manumission, and clientage in a range of legal texts and narrative sources from Mamluk Egypt. I have, for the most part, pushed the military slave into the background in order to shed some light on the domestic slaves, male and female, who were omnipresent in Mamluk urban society. The legal distinction between slave and free was, I argue, one of the most important boundaries in Mamluk society. It was not, however, an impermeable one. Even prior to manumission, the hybrid status of the slave as both person and thing allowed him or her to play a variety of roles that crossed that boundary. At the same time, the highly charged language of death and resurrection used to describe slavery and manumission served both to emphasize the vulnerability of the slave and to valorize the relationship of clientage between former master and former slave.

Yvonne Seng draws upon the rich resource of the Ottoman shariʿa court records to provide us a window into the daily life of slave and free in sixteenth century Üsküdar, a suburb of Istanbul. On the one hand, we see the objectification of the slave as property, along with packhorses, chickens, rugs, and houses, in the estate inventories of the deceased. But this "static definition of status," Seng argues, obscures the dynamic role played by slaves in Ottoman society. Drawing upon the work of Victor Turner, Seng makes use of the concepts of liminality and rites of passage to describe slavery in the context of local communities. The most important aspect of slavery thus becomes the transition of the slave from property, or "property with voice" in the words of the Ottoman jurists, into a member of the community. For Seng, the definition of slaves as "property with voice" takes on new meaning, for the voices of slaves are indeed present in the court records. She shows that slaves had access to the shariʿa courts and made use of them to actively assert their rights in regard to contracts of manumission against their masters or their masters' heirs.

In Yvonne Seng's article as well as in my own, there is a strong emphasis on the variety of roles played by slaves, on the transformative powers of manumission, and on the integration of the freed slave into Muslim communities. John Hunwick's discussion of the re-enslavement of blacks in Morocco in the sixteenth and seventeenth centuries reminds us that this model of social integration cannot be taken for granted.

The connection between race and slavery in the Muslim Middle East has been and continues to be a complex and controversial subject. According to Muslim jurists, it was not skin color but the perversion of unbelief (*kufr*) that caused the individual to suffer the "death" of enslavement and enter into the unnatural condition of slavery. This was the case in Islamic legal theory. However, as John Hunwick points out, the social reality was more complex. Unlike slaves and former slaves from other ethnic backgrounds, black Africans were clearly identifiable. Their very presence in the Muslim Middle East "was largely attributable to slavery, and thus to former unbelief." Black skin thus came to be equated with the sin of unbelief and the status of slavery.

Muslim jurists in North and West Africa were themselves cognizant of and deeply troubled by the tensions between legal theory and social attitudes. The questions posed to Aḥmad Bābā of Timbuktu make it clear that in North and West Africa in the sixteenth century, black Africans were considered "inherently deserving of being enslaved by non-black peoples" regardless of their status as Muslims. The continued protests of members of the ulama against the indiscriminate enslavement of black Africans late into the nineteenth century point to deeply entrenched social attitudes that prevailed in opposition to the "idealism of the shariʿa."

Three of the articles in this volume make use of a range of legal sources. In my article, I have attempted a close reading of the normative language of Muslim jurists. By bringing in material from other kinds of sources such as biographical dictionaries and chronicles, I have tried to place that language in its broader social context. Yvonne Seng's use of shariʿa court records allows us to witness the day-to-day practice of Islamic law. These records confirm the widespread use of Islamic legal institutions like the *kitāba*, the contract for manumission between master and slave. They also give us an intimate portrait of the ways in which real people negotiated those institutions.

In the fatwas used by John Hunwick we see the juncture, or rather the disjuncture, between the theory and practice of Islamic law in North Africa on the issue of enslavement. The voices of the jurists, however, are not the voices of isolated theorists. These were men who were deeply engaged in their communities, who believed in the institution of slavery, and who were not themselves free of racial stereotypes toward black Africans. However, they bitterly opposed the enslavement of Muslims based on skin color as a clear violation of the shariʿa. Hunwick gives us the voices of their opponents as well. The result is a rich and textured analysis of both attitudes toward race and slavery and actual social practices.

Michel LeGall's translation of the memoirs of the French physician Louis Frank on the trade in black Africans in Cairo in the early nineteenth century gives us the perspective of an outsider with little or no knowledge of Islamic law. But Frank understands that slaves are, indeed, property. They are not simply "adopted" outsiders. At the same time, he recognizes the possibility for the slave to be assimilated into Egyptian society through learning a trade, through marriage, and through manumission. Frank's interest, however, lies not in the social context of slavery but in the bodies of the slaves. Thus, we have detailed descriptions of physiognomy, scarification, genital mutilation, castration, and disease. The enslaved black Africans are objects to be catalogued. The catalogue itself is an interesting combination of ethnographic detail and racial stereotypes.

There can be no single model for the study of slavery in Islamic societies. The articles in the present collection shed significant light on the complexity of this institution in both theory and practice and its on multifaceted presence in pre-modern Islamic societies.

Shaun E. Marmon
Princeton University

Domestic Slavery in the Mamluk Empire: A Preliminary Sketch

SHAUN E. MARMON

Although chattel slavery played an integral role in Muslim societies in the Middle East for more than a thousand years, this particular institution has, until recently, received only minimal attention from specialists in Middle Eastern social history.[1] For the Medieval period, in particular, the aspect of Islamic slavery that has attracted the most attention from specialists has been military slavery, the recruitment and training of an armed elite. The masses of non-military slaves—from cooks and concubines to artisans and merchants—remain, for the most part, unstudied.

The following essay, based primarily on Mamluk legal texts and chronicles, is intended to serve as an introduction to a more detailed study of domestic slavery in the Mamluk period. My purpose in this preliminary sketch is to present the ways in which some Mamluk authors understood the condition of slavery, a condition which they, like Orlando Patterson, described as a kind of social death.[2]

The Line Between the Free and the Unfree

Ibn Manẓūr (d. 711/1311), author of the thirteenth century Arabic dictionary, *Lisān al-ʿArab*, cautioned his readers—in his entry for the word *ʿabd* or slave—against confusing the two plurals: *ʿibād*, the worshippers or "slaves" of God, and *ʿabīd*, actual chattel slaves. Every human being, free or slave, Ibn Manẓūr piously affirmed, was an *ʿabd* in the sense that he was in a servile state (*marbūb*) in relationship to his Creator. The "Lord of all worshippers (*ʿibād*) as well as of slaves (*ʿabīd*)" had seen fit, however, to designate some people as worshippers or "slaves" for God (*ʿibād l'illāh*) and others as slaves for both God and His creatures (*l'illāh wa-li'l-makhlūqīn*). These latter were the chattel slaves, the *ʿabīd mamālīk*, the slaves of the slaves of God.[3]

The distinction between slave and free was one of the most crucial legal demarcations within the Muslim community. Muslim Jurists did maintain that "the basic principle is freedom," *al-aṣl huwwa al-ḥurriyya*, and employed this principle to declare foundlings of unknown origin to be free children.[4] This concept did not, however, conflict with their perception of slavery as a divinely ordained institution which separated the owners from the "owned." Pious exhortations to free men to address their slaves by such euphemistic terms as "my boy," *fatayya*, and "my girl," *fatātī*, sprang from the belief that God, not their masters, was responsible for the slave's status. All men might be metaphorical "slaves of God" but the true slave, in the legal sense of the term, was the "owned one, the opposite of the free man," *al-mamlūk khilāf al-ḥurr*. The importance of this distinction becomes evident in the pages of any medieval Islamic legal text: it is very difficult to select randomly a discussion of commercial law, laws of personal status, or penal law without encountering some question relating to slavery or manumission. M. I. Finley's comment on the role of slavery in classical civilization could easily be applied, in this respect, to the civilization of the medieval Middle East:

> . . . there was no action or belief or institution in Graeco-Roman antiquity that was not one way or other affected by the possibility that someone involved might be a slave. It follows that slavery cannot be abstracted from its context.[5]

Slave status, like the status of women, was never a mere question of theory; it was a practical matter with serious legal consequences that could not be overlooked. Given the political system of Mamluk Egypt, one might assume that, for the military slaves at least, the line between free and unfree became somewhat blurred. This is not what the sources reveal. The Turkish and Circassian amirs who formed Egypt's ruling elite were not slaves: they were freedmen and this distinction, in their eyes and in the eyes of legal scholars, was a vital one. More than one highly-placed amir was forced to undergo a second sale and manumission because his original manumission had either never taken place or had been declared invalid post facto on the basis of some legal technicality.[6] Ibn Ḥajar (d. 852/1449), commenting on one such event, was particularly struck by the fact that the amir in question had enjoyed the false status of a free man for so many years: "that was considered very bizarre (*ʿudda min al-gharāʾib*) . . . for Aytmish had lived seventeen years in slavery (*fīʾl-riqq*) while independently exercising the powers of free men (*yataṣarrifu taṣarruf al-aḥrār*) until he became one of the greatest amirs in Egypt."[7]

The enslaved individual suffered a kind of legal and social metamorphosis. He left the realm of human beings and entered the realm of commodities (*al-silaʿ*) thus losing his legal capacity (*ahliyya*) to act of and for himself. Consequently, he had no inherent right to initiate marriage, to own property, to act as a witness, to inherit or to bequeath, to hold any position of authority, or to contract and dispose in commercial matters.

A strong pious tradition, supported by Prophetic *ḥadīth*, constantly exhorted Muslim masters to treat their slaves with kindness. The slave, however, as a legally impotent being, had no capacity to sue his owner for bodily harm. Slavery meant "ownership of the physical person" of the slave, *milk al-raqaba*, and such ownership implied virtually unlimited rights. Such proverbs as "the slave is to be beaten, a hint suffices for the free man" point towards a harsh reality.[8] Ibn Taghrī Birdī (d. 874/1470) speculated that the deposed Sultan al-Manṣūr, who continued to live in the Cairo Citadel during the second reign of Sultan Barqūq, had been poisoned by his female slaves because of his excessive cruelty towards them. Whenever Sultan Barqūq would hear the screams of al-Manṣūr's slave girls, he would intercede on their behalf and al-Manṣūr, fearful of the Sultan's authority, would be forced to cease his abuse. For Ibn Taghrī Birdī, al-Manṣūr's lack of self-control in dealing with his slaves is another example of the "evil character" of the deposed ruler. Likewise, Barqūq's acts of mercy on behalf of the slaves are presented as laudable ones.[9] The fact remains, however, that the unfortunate slaves in question had no recourse themselves against their master's brutality but were dependent upon the outside interference of a powerful personage.

The "ownership of the physical person" of the slave also included, in the case of female slaves, the master's right to unrestricted sexual access as well as his absolute rights over the slave woman's offspring.[10] If he recognized his slave woman's child as his own, that child and all of her subsequent children would have the status of free and legitimate heirs. Such children belonged to their father's kinship group and the right to their *ḥaḍāna* or care devolved upon the father's free female relatives, not upon the slave mother. The mother earned the status of *umm walad*: she could not be sold during her master's lifetime and would be manumitted automatically upon his death. She could still, however, be rented out as a servant or married off against her will. If her children were not fathered by her master, they were also slaves and were the *ghalla* or "fruit" of their mother and thus also the property of the master. The jurists also denied the slave mother the right to *ḥaḍāna* over her slave children.[11]

The role of the female slave as a sexual object and as a potential mother of free children was a crucial one. The primacy of this role is made quite clear by the fact that the statement "your sexual organ is free," *farjuki ḥurrun*, serves as a formula of manumission for female slaves.[12] Likewise, bad breath, body odor, and a propensity for fornication (*zināʾ*) each constitute a fault or *ʿayb* which can serve to cancel the sale of a female slave. Such faults, according to one Hanāfī commentator, interfere with the purpose of the female slave (*al-maqṣūd fīhā*), which is "sexual service and childbearing" (*al-istifrāsh wa-ṭalab al-walad*), while they do not interfere with the purpose of the male slave, which is simply service (*al-istikhdām*).[13]

Sexual exploitation of young male slaves was not within the master's legal rights. The slave boy as sexual object was, however, widely celebrated in Medieval Arabic literature. The jurists decry homoerotic relationships between master and slave but recognize that such relationships exist.[14]

The author of the *Lisān* stated that the "principle of slavery is self-abasement and submission," *aṣl al-ʿubudiyyati huwwa al-tadhallul wa'l-khuḍuʿ*.[15] The legal scholar al-Babārtī (d. 786/1384) described the slave as "legally dead" (*hālik ḥukman*) since "he has no right to many of the powers (*aḥkām*) that are associated with the living."[16] Al-ʿAynī (d. 855/1451) defined slavery as a "legal weakness (*ḍuʿf sharʿī*) which is established on the object of slavery and which makes him incapable of contracting and disposing and takes away his legal capacity (*ahliyya*) in such matters as judgeship, witnessing, authority (*al-salṭana*), and the initiating of marriage (*tazwīj*)."[17] The terms most commonly employed by jurists when describing the status of the slave are those that imply helplessness and deficiency such as *ʿajz*, "impotence," *naqṣ*, "lack" or "defect," *ḍuʿf*, "weakness," and *hulk*, "death." Such legal metaphors made the position of the slave quite clear: he was an "incomplete" and vulnerable being.

No matter how broad the rights granted to the master, no system of chattel slavery has ever succeeded in consistently relegating the slave to the absolute and unmitigated status of "thing." Muslim jurists, as we have seen, basically perceived the slave as a commodity. They did not, however, perceive enslavement as the final termination of the slave's humanity in all situations. Most legal scholars, for example, concurred that while the master was not legally bound to provide adequate physical maintenance or *nafaqa* for his animals, he was required to do so for his slaves. His treatment of his animals was "between him and God Almighty" but his slaves, in contrast, were *min ahl al-istiḥaqq*, "people with a claim," and this claim included proper food and clothing. In their suggestions for enforcement of the slave's right to maintenance, the jurists were, however, careful not to infringe upon the master's right of ownership.

Al-ʿAynī recommended two possible solutions to the problem of a master who did not maintain his slaves. In the case of a male slave who was employed, he could be allowed to keep his earnings and maintain himself. The female slave, the elderly male slave, and the infirm slave should, however, be sold:

> . . . for they are among the people with a claim (*min ahl al-istiḥaqq*) and in sale lies the fulfillment of their claim and it does not cancel the claim of the master because the proceeds of the sale takes their place.[18]

The most significant recognition of the slave's humanity occurs in the Islamic laws of marriage and divorce. Unlike many other slave-holding societies, Muslim society recognized the validity of slave marriages. The male slave could marry only half the number of wives granted to a free man and he could not initiate marriage without his master's consent. The jurists were, however, divided as to whether the master possessed the right of coercion or *ijbār* in marriage over his male slaves as he did over his female slaves and minor children.[19]

The special status of the male slave in relationship to marriage stands out very clearly in discussions of divorce. Under no circumstance could the master impose a divorce upon his married male slaves, because the "ownership of marriage (*milk al-nikāḥ*), is the right of the slave and its abrogation (*isqāṭ*) belongs to him, not to the master."[20] The commentary of al-Babārtī on this subject is particularly interesting: "this is because the *milk* of marriage is one of the special attributes (*khaṣā'iṣ*) of human beings (*al-adāmiyya*) and the slave still posesses this attribute because of the original principle of freedom, *ʿala aṣl al-ḥurriyya*."[21]

The jurists, by granting the male slave practically the same rights to divorce as a free man, conceded two points that obviously conflicted with the slave's status as a commodity. The first and most obvious one was that the slave, despite his legal metamorphosis from person to thing, retained certain "natural" or "original" human qualities. The second point, one that had far-reaching consequences in the realm of commercial activity, was that slavery did not, in itself, destroy the slave's natural capacity for ownership or *milk* since he remained capable of *milk* in marriage.

Like the minor and the insane, the slave was generally recognized to be in a state of *hajr* or "legal restriction" in regards to his capacity (*ahliyya*) to contract and dispose. This, however, could easily be lifted by the permission or *idhn* of the master, a practice reflected in the important institution of the *ma'dhūn* slave who could stand, as it were, in the place of his master as the latter's business agent. The *ma'dhūn* slave not only served his master's commercial interests; he also conducted business for himself. This facile removal of *hajr* implied that the restriction, in the first place, had been artificial and that the slave had never really lost his original capacity to contract and dispose. That capacity had been "suspended," so to speak, by slavery. This seems to be the import of the following comments by al-ʿAynī:

> Slavery (*al-riqq*) is not, in reality, a true cause of *hajr* since

> the slave may be legally competent (*mukallif*), in need (*muḥtāj*) and of sound mind (*kāmil al-rayy*) like the free man except that he and what he possesses are in the ownership of his master. Because of this it is not permissible for him to act for himself. Once the slave becomes *ma'dhūn,* however, this situation is completely reversed. In the Holy Law, *idhn* is the dissolution of *hajr* and the abrogation of the right (of the master) because the slave would be capable of contracting and disposing even after enslavement were it not for the *hajr* which is upon him because of the right (*ḥaqq*) of his master. If the master grants him his *idhn,* he loses his right and the slave becomes competent to exercise his original capacity (*ahliyyatuhu al-aṣliyya*).[22]

The most important result of *idhn* was that the slave could, in a sense, own property for "the master of the *ma'dhūn* does not own what is in the possession (*fī yad*) of the *ma'dhūn.*"[23] Some legal scholars even held that if a master saw his slave engaged in some sort of commercial activity and remained silent, his silence in itself was a tacit grant of *idhn.* Likewise, an adult male slave of sound mind and body who was not receiving adequate support from his master was expected to seek employment of some sort in order to feed and clothe himself.[24]

The institution of the *kitāba*, like that of *idhn*, also introduced a great deal of flexibility into the slave system. Any slave could enter into a contract of *kitāba* with his master for his freedom, provided, of course, that his master was amenable to the idea. This contract usually involved a guarantee on the part of the slave to provide a certain sum of money or certain services over a specified period of time in exchange for his freedom.

The *kitāba* signified a drastic change in status for the slave: he remained in the *milk* or ownership of his master but was no longer in his possession or *yad*. What this meant for the slave was that he now had the right to retain his own earnings, to contract and dispose in commercial matters, and even to own slaves himself. He still could not contract a marriage without his master's consent and was legally barred from witnessing, judgeship, etc., like an average slave. The *mukātib* could not, however, be sold by his master, and he enjoyed a semi-manumitted status. He was considered, according to al-ʿAynī, "to have flown out of the humiliation of slavery (*dhull al-riqq*) but not yet to have alighted upon the open space of freedom."[25]

Manumission served as a strong mitigating factor within the slave system.The slave could earn his own manumission by means of a *kitāba*. The *umm walad*, as we have already mentioned, gained her manumission upon her master's death. Likewise, a slave who was declared *mudabbar* could not be sold during his master's lifetime and was manumitted after the latter's death. Certain degrees of kinship, once discovered, also guaranteed automatic manumission. The manumitted slave suffered no legal disabilities. In theory, manumission completely reversed the metamorphosis caused by slavery. The possibilities of manumission or of a partial change in status undoubtedly served to ease the rather difficult position of the "unfree." The broad powers of the master over his slave as his possession were—in the case of the *mukātib*, the *umm walad*, and the *mudabbar*—significantly curtailed since the master could claim only a restricted ownership over such slaves. Such "mitigating factors" as the *kitāba* and the grant of *idhn* also served to make the slave system more flexible and more responsive to certain economic and social needs, particularly in the realm of commercial activity. The basic status of the slave was still that of a commodity. He was, however, a very special kind of commodity which could perform a variety of important functions. The possibility of restoring his "suspended" humanity through manumission undoubtedly served as a powerful incentive to perform those functions.[26]

The Slave Is He Who Has No Slave

The historian Ibn Taghrī Birdī mentions the deaths of large numbers of slaves in his home during the plague of 834/1430:

> . . . as for those who died in our household among the military slaves (*al-mamālīk*), the black domestic slaves (*al-ʿabīd*), the female slaves (*al-jawārī*), and the eunuchs (*al-khadam*), their number is beyond calculation . . .[27]

The maintenance of such a numerous group of slaves—allowing a certain margin for literary hyperbole—must have been an economic strain upon a family that had supposedly suffered financial disaster with the death of the historian's father, the commander-in-chief of Sultan Faraj's army, the amir Tanri Verdī. What purpose did these slaves serve? Given the military and political connections of the family, the presence of military slaves, *mamālīk*, is no surprise. The non-military slaves probably fulfilled the two most obvious slave-functions in this society: domestic service and, in the case of females, childbearing. Slaves, as maids, cooks, nurses, and valets, took on the burden of day-to-day cooking, cleaning, and childcare. Men who exercised any position of prestige—like Ibn Taghr Bird and his brothers—required *hujjāb* or doormen to screen visitors and petitioners, stable hands (*ghilmān*) to care for riding mounts, and trained entertainers for social functions held at their homes. In a wealthy household, favorite concubines, despite their slave status, did not engage in domestic duties and thus required additional "service" slaves to wait on them. The absence of slaves in a wealthy home was not even considered for, as the poet al-Ghuzūlī put it, "The slave is he who has no slaves" (*al-ʿabd man la ʿabīd lahu*).[28]

Ibn Shahīn's (d. 872/1468) description of the Sultan's harem in the Cairo Citadel gives us a picture of the large numbers of such service slaves in the premier household of the Empire:

> . . . as for the concubines, their number used to be forty. Each concubine had her entourage, her male and female slaves, and her eunuchs. As for the rest of the female slaves in the Noble Dwellings, they constitute a numerous group of women of all races among whom are those who have special occupations . . . for there are bath attendants, wet nurses, and special governesses.[29]

Although few families in Cairo could have afforded such extravagance, the Sultan's household in the Citadel can be viewed as a sort of macrocosm of upper-class domestic life. Tanri Verdī, father of the historian, astonished his own former master, Sultan Barqūq, with a gift of "twenty mamluks and five white eunuchs of great beauty." What surprised the Sultan was that the amir could afford such a gift, despite the expense of maintaining his own numerous slaves.[30] Many of the slaves whom Tanri Verdī acquired from other masters eventually served as important historical informants for his son Yūsuf: among them were the male and female Circassian slaves of Barqūq's deceased sisters, the fifteen skilled singing girls of the Sultan al-Manṣūr, and one of the favorite concubines of the rebellious amir, Iyās.[31]

The reasons for acquiring so many costly slaves were obviously much more complex than the purely practical need for servants and potential mothers. Another proverb quoted by al-Ghuzūlī runs: "Slaves (*al-ʿabīd*), even if they consume your wealth, increase your prestige." Likewise, "the comfortable life lies in the spaciousness of the dwelling and status in the number of slaves."[32]

Slaves, along with certain other possessions, symbolized wealth and power. A government official who went from a position of relative obscurity to that of wazir in the space of one day's time, described his change of fortune in the following terms:

> He (the wazir) used to relate that when he woke up on that day he did not even own a single dirham but by the evening of the same day, the quantity of his horses, mules, camels, property (*māl*), slaves (*mamālīk*), clothes and household utensils surpassed description.[33]

In a similar vein, one of the amirs of Mecca was memorialized in these words: "He was great in leadership (*riyāsa*) and dignity (*ḥishma*), he acquired a great quantity of real estate (*al-ʿaqār*) and of black slaves (*al-ʿabīd*)."[34]

Lists of confiscated goods from the homes of deposed officials frequently included slaves—particularly, it seems, when the historian was trying to emphasize the wealth of the person in question. We read, for example, that "grain, embroidered cloth, and slaves (*raqīq*)" to the value of two million dirhams were found in the home of one fallen official.[35] Another unlucky bureaucrat was forced to surrender "the women (*al-nisāʾ*), the male and female slaves (*al-ghilmān w'al-jawārī*), and the possessions (*al-amwāl*)" in his house—all of which added up to a sum of two hundred thousand dinars.[36] When the unpopular Abū al-Khayr al-Nahhās fell from power in 854/1450, the Sultan immediately demanded that he hand over his forty horses and twenty mamluks to the government.[37]

A large number of slaves signified that a man had both money and position. They also served as a support group for their master in a number of ways. Early ties of loyalty established between free children (whose mothers might well be slaves) and personal slaves could be quite profound. When Barsbay deposed and imprisoned the young son of Sultan Shaʿbān, he allowed the prisoner access to a certain number of intimate slaves and freedmen: the youth's former nurse, his Abyssinian governess, Sirr al-Nadīm, his concubines, and an Indian eunuch named Ṣandal, a freedman of his mother's. These attendants, with the aid of a cook who had been a servant and possibly a freedman of the boy's father, masterminded a daring although unsuccessful escape attempt on behalf of their young master.[38]

Ibn Taghrī Birdī tells a less dramatic but equally significant story about his efforts to arrange a proper funeral for one of his house-born (*muwallada*, possibly "mulatto") slave girls who died during the plague:

> . . . there died in our household a *waṣīfa muwallada*. She fell ill at noon and was dead before sunset. We awoke in the morning and discovered that the servants had not been able to find a coffin for her. Her mother and a group of the old women (*al-ʿajāʾiz*) took charge of washing her body and laying her out in her finest dress with the greatest of care. Meanwhile, we had still not found a coffin for her. It so happened that I had to go out that day to pray over the deceased grand amīr Baybogha al-Muẓaffirī . . . so some of the servants carried the dead girl in their arms while I stood at the entrance of the house until a woman's funeral procession went by. I took down the coffin by force (*ghasban*) and placed her body beside the body of the dead woman and the two were carried off together on the shoulders of the men. Her mother and some of the servants went along until they reached the cemetery, then they removed her from the coffin and buried her.[39]

The presumed bonds of loyalty between master and slave, bonds that went beyond death, often placed the slave in situations of extraordinary danger. Conscious of the "inside knowledge" of most household slaves concerning the details of their masters' lives, the authorities occasionally singled those slaves out for interrogation and torture if the master or, more importantly, the master's wealth was an object of concern for the Sultan.[40] Slaves also suffered from a master's downfall. When Sultan Barqūq was in prison, his sister and her slave girls were dragged through the streets of Cairo unveiled and subjected to abuse by his enemies.[41] The slave girls of a disgraced amir were abducted from his home by an angry mob.[42] The slaves of deposed officials, as we have previously mentioned, were confiscated along with the rest of the unlucky individual's possessions and re-sold.

The same legal and social inferiority that made slaves so vulnerable also made them, in some cases, capable of a certain flexibility of behavior denied to the free. This was particularly true in the case of women. Female slaves were not bound by the same rules of dress and decorum as were free women. When the women of Cairo and Fustat were forbidden to leave their homes during a period of particular moral conservatism, their female slaves (*amāʾ*) went out unveiled to attend to the errands of their mistresses. They were specifically ordered to uncover their faces, however, so that free women would be discouraged from attempting to go out disguised as slaves.[43]

Slave women also played an important and dramatic role as public mourners in the case of the death or disgrace of prominent men. When the son of Sultan Shaʿbān, al-Malik al-ʿAzīz Yūsuf, was finally sent off to prison in Alexandria, the slave women who had belonged to his mother and father gathered at the site of his mother's tomb and held an emotional mourning ceremony, as one historian put it, "weeping and causing others to weep."[44]

For a young slave, a change in masters could mean transfer from one social group to another. Fārīs al-Qutluqjāwī, a freedman and high ranking amir of Sultan Barqūq, was originally the slave of a baker in Alexandria:

> His origin was from among the military slaves of the amīr Khalīl b. ʿArrām, the *nāʾib* of Alexandria, who bought him from a baker (*khabbāz*). Ibn ʿArrām saw the boy and was pleased by him so he purchased him from the baker. Then he (Fāris) came into the possession of al-Malik al-Ẓāhir Barqūq after Ibn ʿArram . . . .[45]

Fāris, as the slave or freedman of the baker. would never have attained the position of power which he eventually enjoyed as a military slave and freedman of Barqūq.

The most important and, from a legal point of view, the most interesting use of slaves by merchants and tradesmen, however, lay in the institution of the *ma'dhūn* slaves. The chronicles present us with interesting confirmation—in practice—of what the legal texts tell us in theoretical terms. Ibn Ḥajar, for example, relates that at one time in Cairo there were some two hundred Karimī merchants who owned some one hundred black slaves (*'abīd*). These slaves engaged in long-distance trade on behalf of their masters.[46] The same historian, in his biographical entry for a wealthy merchant, Muḥammad b. Musallam, comments: "It is said that no black slave of his died in a foreign country (*fi'l-ghurba*). They used to travel about on business but not a single one of them died outside of Egypt—one of them was even gone for twenty years but he returned and died in his master's house."[47] When this merchant died, he did not leave his minor son in the charge of a spendthrift elder brother, but confided him to the care of one of his freedmen, the eunuch Kāfūr. The latter looked after the boy's affairs until he was old enough to manage his own property.[48]

Such accounts of slaves and freedmen in positions of trust reflect the unique role of the slave as a kind of substitute son. Like a grown son, the *ma'dhūn* slave had ties to his master that made him a potentially more trustworthy business agent than someone from outside the master's household. It was not uncommon for a young slave to be taken quite literally as a "substitute son," like the biblical Joseph in the house of Potiphar, by a childless master. Urgun, a boy of Central Asian origin, served this purpose for the amir Sudūn, nephew of Sultan Barqūq: "Sudūn had purchased him and raised him. Then he freed him and married him to his own daughter. He made him his *ustādār*, his *dawādār,* and the manager of his household (*hākim baytihi*)."[49] The pious legal scholar Sa'īd b. 'Abd Allāh al-Ḥabashī began his career as a slave boy of the high-ranking eunuch Bashīr. The latter took a special interest in Sa'īd, educated him, freed him, and ensured him a succession of government posts.[50]

The "substitute son," as long as he remained in the legal status of slavery, was also a disposable son. If he proved unsatisfactory, he could be sold. Unlike a biological son, he had no rights of inheritance. If he were manumitted, his master would have the right to inherit from him but not vice versa. Surviving deeds of *waqf* in Cairo do contain many provisions for pensions for manumitted slaves or for slaves on the condition that they are manumitted by a certain date. The master, the founder of the *waqf*, had the right, however, to cancel such provisions at any time prior to his own death. It is clear, however, that manumission created a much more powerful bond between master and former slave and incorporated the free slave into a more secure social network.

Manumission and Clientage

Just as the slave was perceived to be in a state of legal death (*al-raqīq hālik hukman*), manumission (*al-ʿitq, al-ʿitāqa*)—the action that gave birth to clientage—was often described as a resurrection.[51] The manumittor gave life to his slave (*aḥyāhu*) by removing his servile status (*bi-izālati al-riqq ʿanhu*).[52] Manumission thus established a legal strength (*quwwatun sharʿiyyatun*) that made up for the weakness (*ḍuʿf*) of slavery.[53] The freedman was restored to complete human status and the rights of all other men over his person were cancelled. He had gained a salvation (*takhlīṣ*) from the humiliation of ownership of the physical person (*dhull milk al-raqaba*) and, in all respects, he was now the juridical equal of the freeborn man.[54] Given this positive transformation, it is not surprising that the author of the *Lisān al-ʿArab* defined manumission as "the best benefit which one person can bestow upon another (*afḍal ma yunʿim aḥadun ʿala aḥadin*) for he (the manumittor) releases him from slavery, he makes up by manumission for his (the slave's) deficiency (*naqṣ*) and perfects for him the powers of free men in all activities (*aḥkām al-aḥrār fī jamīʿi al-taṣarrufāt*)."[55]

The use of such legal language served to emphasize the benevolent nature of manumission—often referred to as a *niʿma*, "grace" or "benefit"—and to reinforce constantly the freedman's sense of obligation. Religious tradition encouraged manumission as an act of piety that would weigh in the master's favor on the Day of Judgment and Islamic law offered the master several methods by which to bestow this *niʿma* on his slave. The apparent frequency of manumission may not have lain so much in pious benevolence but in the powerful role played by clientage, *walāʾ*, in Mamluk society. Al-ʿAynī gave the following definition for the word *walāʾ* in his legal commentary:

> It is a derivative of *al-walāya,* which means support and affection, because there is mutual support and affection in the *walāʾ* of manumission . . . or it is derived from *waliy,* which means closeness (*qurb*), for *walāʾ* is a legal kinship (*qarrābatun hukmiyatun*) that results from the act of manumission . . . or it is from *al-muwāla,* which means continuance, because in the *walāʾ* of manumission there is inheritance (*irth*) . . .. In the *sharīʿa*, the *walāʾ* of manumission signifies mutual support (*tanāṣur*) . . . its results are inheritance (*irth*) and payment of the blood money (*ʿaql*) . . .[56]

Prior to manumission, the slave was basically a kinless being—a true outsider. Although jurists condemned the separation of minor slaves from their mothers or from close relatives, they did not declare such sales invalid. Most slaves, in any case, had already been separated from their families when they were seized or purchased somewhere in their country of origin. The very use of the term *mawla* for both patron and client served to emphasize the artificial kinship created by manumission. A commonly repeated legal adage was the "the relationship of clientage becomes like the relationship between father and son" (*al-walāʾ yasīru ka'l-wilād*).[57] The author of the *Lisān* pointed out that one meaning of the plural *al-mawālī* was "paternal cousins" (*banī al-ʿamm*) and that the manumitted slave takes the place of the paternal cousin. Manumitted slaves were also called *al-mawālī*, he added, because "the *mawla* is the manumitted one (*al-muʿtaq*) who becomes affiliated with your kinship group (*intasaba bi-nasabika*)."[58]

The only person who could establish clientage with a former slave was his manumittor (*al-walāʾ li-man ʿataqa*).[59] Previous masters had no claim upon the slave other than whatever personal obligations he might feel toward them. Once manumission was complete, neither the master nor the freedman could transfer this relationship to any third party. A *ḥadīth* from the Prophet—quoted and re-quoted—stated this provision quite forcefully: "Clientage is a relationship like the relationship of kinship, it cannot be sold or given away" (*al-walāʾ luhma ka-luhmat al-nasab lam yubāʾ wa-lam yuwhab*).[60]

The former slave, deracinated by the "death" of enslavement, was now the *mawla*, the "legal kinsman" of his patron and could expect a certain degree of social and legal support from his patron's family. Although his given name, like the fanciful Yāqūt or "Ruby," was a recognizable slave name, he adopted a *nisba* taken from his manumittor. His manumittor, in turn, could now count one more person among the members of his own support group—a man or woman who was eternally bound to him and to his children by a profound sense of obligation for his or her "resurrection" from the death of slavery.

The Relationship between Patron and Client

The relationship between Ibn Musallam, the wealthy merchant, and his freed eunuch, Kāfūr, is a paradigmatic one in Mamluk texts. After Ibn Musallam's death, the devoted Kāfūr raised the boy and looked after his affairs until he was old enough to assume the management of his own.[61] Yāqūt al-Kamālī Ibn al-Barizī, freedman of the Ibn al-Barizī family of religious scholars and government officials in Cairo, took on the care of the children and grandchildren of his manumittor.

> He (Yāqūt) devoted himself to his patron's service and after his death, he was with his (former) master's daughter in the house of al-Jamālī, the *nāẓir al-khaṣṣ*. He undertook the upbringing of her sons, especially al-Kamālī (al-Kamāl Muḥammad, grandson of Yāqūt's patron), the *nāẓir al-jaysh*, and later of al-Kamālī's son. Indeed, he was the educator (*al-murabbī*) of most of his patron's children. He went on the *hajj* and he was intelligent, religious, and peaceful, a lover of goodness and good people . . . . He died at the age of seventy years or more.[62]

These bonds of affection established with the children of the patron's family obviously worked both ways: the Shafiʿī legal scholar, Taqī al-Dīn as-Subkī, was reportedly devoted to his father's freedman Miftāḥ, and, as Ibn Ḥajar put it, "Taqī al-Dīn used to depend upon him and his (Miftāḥ's) word was law with him."[63] Freedmen who were of the same age as their master's children had often received their own education alongside them. Tay Boga al-Sharīfī was a well-known calligrapher, *ḥadīth* scholar, teacher, and professional witness who began his career as the young slave of the sharif Shihāb al-Dīn, the *naqīb al-ashrāf* in Aleppo. This eminently successful freedman had "learned *ḥadīth* with the sharif's children from al-Jamāl Ibn al-Shihāb Maḥmūd and learned calligraphy with them from the shaykh Ḥasan and he excelled in his beautiful handwriting."[64] Freedmen-scholars, as one might expect, were almost always the clients of ulama families from whom they received both an education and the necessary social connections to pursue their own careers. Yāqūt al-Ḥabashī al-Fahadī, the former slave of the Ibn al-Fahad family in Mecca, was himself a highly respected scholar, lauded for his excellent character. When Yāqūt died, he was buried in his patron's family tomb and Ibn al-Fahad included him in a biographical dictionary of scholars.[65]

It is no coincidence that the freedmen who merited an entry in a biographical dictionary or in the yearly lists of obituaries of important men in chronicles were invariably the clients of high-status families of government officials, scholars, and wealthy merchants. Such freedmen were more likely to have educational opportunities and a chance to establish their own careers. The freedmen of religious scholars, as we have illustrated, often became scholars themselves. Likewise, the freedmen of merchants would be likely to make their living through commerce. Among the latter we find "Yāqūt al-Rahabī, one of the freedmen of the wealthy merchants who was known for his good character. He owned more than one ship on the sea."[66]

More important, however, than the freedman's expectation of pursuing a career related to the career of his patron, was the prestige of clientage with a respected family. The case of the freedman who served as tutor to three generations of the Ibn al-Barizī family is a clear example of the reflection of the patron's status on the client. Many freedmen may have played similar roles but they did not earn a place in al-Sakhāwī's biographical dictionary.

Conclusion

In ideal circumstances, the individual who suffered the "death" of enslavement would be "resurrected" to a new Muslim identitity through manumission.[67] Pseudo-kinship is not, however, real kinship. Not all slaves were manumitted and not all manumitted slaves could depend upon their master's playing the role of benevolent patron. The discussion of slavery in the context of family law may say as much about the hierarchical structure of families as it does about the relationships between masters and slaves.

The question of the maintenance or *nafaqa* of slaves, for example, is dealt with in the same chapter of most legal texts that deals with the *nafaqa* of wives, children, and other dependent relatives. The most striking legal correlation between slavery and family relationships, however, lies in the jurists' constant pairing of divorce and manumission. Discussions of oaths (*īmān*) generally include oaths relating to divorce and manumission under the same heading. When the Malikī jurist Ibn Qayyim al-Jawziyya wrote a treatise on the question of divorce initiated in a moment of anger (*ṭalāq al-ghadbān*), he also included the question of manumission under similar circumstances.[68] This correlation also appears in the order of the chapters of many medieval legal commentaries, since the "Book of Manumission," *kitāb al-ʿitāq*, generally follows directly after the "Book of Divorce," *kitāb al-ṭalāq*. The fifteenth-century commentator al-ʿAynī gave the following explanation for this standard order:

> The reason for the analogy between the two books lies in the fact that divorce is the release of the individual from the subjugation of ownership of the sexual organ (*takhlīṣ al-shakhṣ min dhull milk al-mutʿa*) and manumission is the release of the individual from the subjugation of ownership of the physical person (*takhlīṣ al-shakhṣ min dhull milk al-raqaba*).[69]

This passage makes clear that the real analogy does not lie between divorce, which is a sort of repudiation, and manumission, which initiates a new and more profound relationship, but between marriage and slavery—both of which involve a kind of *milk* or ownership. The husband pays a certain sum to his prospective wife through her *wali* or guardian and thus acquires the right to exclusive sexual access, the right to claim her offspring as members of his kinship group, and the right to exercise a fairly broad control over her person and her activities. The jurists described this transaction as resulting in a *milk* or ownership of the woman's sexual organ: "*nikāḥ* (marriage) is a contract, the purpose of which is ownership of sexual access." Likewise, the sale and donation of slaves were described as contracts the purpose of which was ownership of the physical person. Such contracts, according to al-ʿAynī, were distinct from marriage in that the direct purpose of marriage was *milk al-mutʿa* and the purpose of transactions involving slaves was *milk al-raqaba,* which might incidentally include *milk al-mutʿa.*[70] Just as the master of a slave possessed the exclusive right of manumission, the husband alone could initiate divorce "because the man is the owner (*al-malik*) and he has, as it were, enslaved the woman through the dowry (*huwwa ka ʿl-mustariqq lahā biʿl-mahr*) and because she has no discernment in her affairs."[71]

This does not mean of course that marriage, which involved a social bond between two families as well as certain legal obligations on the part of the husband, was the exact equivalent of purchasing a slave. The free wife had rights over her own property and she had her own kinship connections—a father, brothers, and male cousins who could presumably exert pressure on a negligent or abusive husband. Unlike the slave, she was not a social outsider.

A common medieval Arabic proverb, quoted by al-Ghuzūlī, states, "It is better to raise a slave than a son, for the son generally sees his advantage in his father's death and the slave sees his advantage in the continued existence of his master."[72] Among all the dependents of a free man, his slaves were certainly the most dependent—not only because they were physically in his power, but because they were deracinated and kinless people. If the master chose to manumit the slave, he cemented this dependency forever by making the slave into his fictional kinsman—a kinsman whose burden of obligation, however, was in some ways more profound than that of any blood kinsman.

Notes

1. For brief overviews of slavery in medieval Islam see R. Bruschvig, s.v. "ʿAbd," *Encyclopaedia of Islam*, 2nd edition (Leiden: E. J. Brill, 1954–) and S. Marmon, s.v. "Slavery, Islamic," *Dictionary of the Middle Ages* (New York: Charles Scribner & Sons, 1982–89). See also Bernard Lewis, *Race and Slavery in the Middle East, An Historical Inquiry* (New York: Oxford University Press, 1992). For two important studies based on documents, see Donald Little, "Six Fourteenth-Century Purchase Deeds for Slaves from al-Haram as-Sharif" in *Zeitschrift der Deutschen Morgenländischen Gesellschaft* 131 (1981), 297–337 and "Two Fourteenth-Century Court Records from Jerusalem Concerning the Disposition of Slaves by Minors," *Arabica* 29 (1982), 16–49.

2. Orlando Patterson, *Slavery and Social Death: A Comparative Study* (Cambridge, MA: Harvard University Press, 1982).

3. Ibn Manẓūr, *Lisān al-ʿArab* (Beirut, 1374/1955), 3:270b, s.v. *ʿabd*: "the *ʿabd* is the human being (*al-insān*) free or slave because he is in a state of servitude to his Lord (*marbūb li-rabbihi*)"; "al-Azhārī said: the people in general came to an agreement to differentiate between the *ʿibād lillāh* and the *mamālīk* and they said, 'This is an *ʿabd* from the *ʿibād lillāh* and these are *ʿabīd mamālīk*.'" Also, "the one who has a right to this is God Almighty who is the Lord of all *ʿibād* and *ʿabīd* . . . He made some of them *ʿibād lillāh* and others from the community he made (slaves) to God and to his creatures (*l'il-lāh wa li'l-makhlūqīn*)," 3:271a.

4. See R. Brunschvig, "ʿAbd," *EI2*, 3:26a; F. Rosenthal, *The Muslim Concept of Freedom*, p. 32. See al-ʿAynī, *Sharḥ al-kanz* (Cairo, 1312 A.H.), 1:271 for a characteristic defense of the free status of the foundling.

5. M.I. Finley, *Ancient Slavery and Modern Ideology* (New York, 1980, reprinted Princeton, 1998), p. 133.

6. For examples of amirs who were subjected to a second sale, see Ibn Taghrī Birdī, *al -Nujūm al-ẓāhira fī mulūk miṣr wa'l-Qāhira*, ed. William Popper, 5 vols. (Berkeley: University of California Press, 1909–36), 6:344; Ibn al-Khaṭīb al-Jawhārī, *Nuzhat al-nufūs wa'l-abdān fī tawārīkh al-zamān*, ed. Hasan Habashī, 3 vols. (Cairo, 1974), 1:80; Ibn Ḥajar al-ʿAsqalānī, *Inbāʾ al-ghumr bi-anbāʾ al-ʿumr*, ed. Hasan Habashī, 4 vols. (Cairo, 1969–72), 1:278.

7. Ibn Hajar, 1:278.

8. Al-Qalqashandī, *Ṣubḥ al-aʾshā fī ṣināʿat al-inshāʾ*, 14 vols. (Cairo, 1913–20, rpt. Cairo, 1963) 1:304. Quoted in Franz Rosenthal, *The Muslim Concept of Freedom* (Leiden, 1960), p. 95. See Rosenthal, n. 300, for several other citations of this proverb.

9. *Nujūm*, 5:505–506.

10. For a brief overview of the status of the slave concubine in Medieval Islam, see S. Marmon, s.v. "Concubinage, Islamic," *Dictionary of the Middle Ages*. Working independently, Baber Johansen and I have used some of the same legal texts to explore the differences in the legal construction of the male and female slave in Sunni law. See Baber Johansen, "The Valorization of the Human Body in Sunni Law," *Princeton Papers: Interdisciplinary Journal of Middle Eastern Studies* 4 (Spring 1996): 71–112.

11. Al-ʿAynī, 1:189, maintains that the *umm walad* and the ordinary female slave are incapable of caring for their children because they are occupied with "service to the master."

12. Ibid., 1:189; cf. Ibn al-Humām al-Sīwāsī, *Sharḥ fatḥ al-qadīr* (Cairo 1389/1970), 4:434–35.

13. Al-ʿAynī, 2:13–14; al-Suyūṭī, however, in his concise *Kitāb al-ashbāh wa'l-naẓā'ir* (Cairo, 1964), p. 483, lists "fornication, stealing, running away, and bad breath issuing from the stomach" as flaws in a slave regardless of gender.

14. Ibn Qayyim al-Jawziyya maintains that a slave is justified in running away from his master in order to avoide pederasty (*liwāṭ*). See *al-Ṭurūq al-hukumiyya fī al-siyāsa al-sharʿiyya* (Medina, 1971), p. 54.

15. *Lisān*, 3:271a.

16. Al-Babārtī, *Sharḥ al-ʿināya ʿala al-hidāya*, printed in the margins of Ibn al-Humām al-Sīwasī, *Sharḥ fatḥ al-qadīr*, 7:283.

17. Al-ʿAynī, 1:196.

18. Al-ʿAynī, 1:196.

19. Al-ʿAynī, 1:134, argued that the master had the right of coercion. He did point out, however, that Abū Yūsuf, Abū Hānīfa, and al-Shafiʿī were all opposed to coercion of the male slave into marriage. This is also the opinion put forward by al-Suyūṭī, p. 249, "He is not to be coerced [into marriage] whether he is a child or an adult."

20. This was al-Marghīnānī's formulation in the sixth/twelfth century. It was quoted and re-quoted by subsequent Hanafi jurists. See Ibn al-Humām al-Sīwāsī, *Sharḥ fatḥ al-qadīr* (Cairo, 1970) 3:493; al-Babārtī, 3:493.

21. Al-Babārtī adds, however, "if we have stated by this something that is harmful to the master, we abandon this principle for his sake." Ibid.

22. Al-ʿAynī, 2:182.

23. Ibid., 2:186.

24. Ibn al-Humām, 4:478.

25. Al-ʿAynī, 2:169.

26. For a nuanced discussion of the importance of slaves as "contract" laborers, see Yvonne Seng, "A Liminal State: Slavery in Sixteenth-Century Istanbul," in this volume.

27. *Nujūm*, 6:665.

28. Al-Ghuzūlī, *Matāliʿ al-budūr fī manāzil al-surūr* (Cairo, 1300 A.H.), 1:29–34, 246–258, 258–66, on the various types of slaves who serve as entertainers, sexual partners, and servants in the ideal home.

29. Ibn Shahīn al-Ẓāhirī, *Kitāb zubdat kashf al-mamālik*, ed. Paul Ravaisse (Paris, 1894), p. 12.

30. *Nujūm*, 5:576.

31. *Nujūm*, 5:366, on Barqūq's Circassian slaves; 5:506, on the singing girls of al-Manṣūr; 5:635, on the concubine of Iyās. Yusūf's father had children by at least two of these women and all of them later served as informants for his son in the course of his historical research.

32. Al-Ghuzūlī, 1:258.

33. Ibn Ḥajar, 2:89.

34. Ibid., 1:320.

35. Ibid., 1:320.

36. Ibid., 1:402–403.

37. Al-Khaṭīb al-Jawhārī, 1:77.

38. *Nujūm*, 7:70–73.

39. Ibid., 6:657.

40. See Ibn Ḥajar, 1:207, on the arrest and torture of a slave in an effort to find his master who was in hiding. Cf. 1:198.

41. *Nujūm*, 5:492.

42. Ibid., 5:584.

43. Ibid., 6:761.

44. Ibid., 7:106.

45. Ibid., 6:343.

46. Ibn Ḥajar, 1:196.

47. Ibid., 1:99.

48. Ibid.

49. Ibid., 1:533.

50. Ibid., 2:528.

51. For a masterful study of the origins of clientage in early Islam, see Patricia Crone, *Roman, Provincial and Islamic Law, The Origins of the Islamic Patronate* (Cambridge University Press: Cambridge, 1987).

52. Ibn al-Humām and al-Babārtī, citing al-Marghīnānī, 7:282.

53. Al-ʿAynī, 1:196.

54. Ibid.

55. *Lisān*, 10:235a.

56. Al-ʿAynī, 2:178.

57. Ibn al-Humām and al-Babārtī, 7:282.

58. *Lisān*, 14:408.

59. Al-ʿAynī, 2:187.

60. See Crone, p. 40.

61. Ibn Ḥajar, 1:199.

62. Al-Sakhāwī, *al-Ḍawʾ al-lāmiʿ fī aʿyān al-qarn al-tāsiʿ*, 12 vols. (Cairo, 1934–36), 10:213.

63. Ibn Ḥajar, 2:129.

64. Ibid., 2:258.

65. Al-Sakhāwī, 10:213.

66. Ibid., 10:214.

67. On the subject of manumission as social integration, see Yvonne Seng's contribution to this volume.

68. Ibn Qayyim al-Jawziyya, *Ighāthat al-lahfān fī hukm ṭalāq al-ghadbān* (Cairo, 137 A.H.), passim.

69. Al-ʿAynī, 1:196.

70. Ibid., 1:115.

71. Ibid.

72. Al-Ghuzūlī, 1:246.

A Liminal State: Slavery in Sixteenth-Century Istanbul

YVONNE SENG

In mid-Cemaziyelâhır 927 (late May 1520), the evaluator for the court district of Üsküdar, a suburb of Istanbul, walked through the house of the learned gentleman Şaban Halife bin Mustafa, enumerating the possessions of the deceased and awarding them a fair market price (2:129a).[1] Part way through the assessment of this *tereke* or *muhallefat,* he left the stable and entered the house. At this point his inventory read ". . . a packhorse, 240 akçe; a slave by name of Süleyman, 2,200 akçe; a tray (*tepsi*), 8; a cup (*tas*), 6; a rug (*kaliçe*), 155. . ." Süleyman the slave was frozen in situ between stable and house, captured in mid-duty.[2] Similarly, in 1528 a female slave with the felicitous name of "Tutu" was listed in the estate of Mehmet bin Yunus, in Gece quarter (6.33b). Valued at 2,000 akçe, her presence was recorded after a series of domestic items—a box of pears, another box with flour inside, some chickens, and grass matting used as an enclosure—but before the most valuable item, a house with an orchard (3,000 akçe).[3]

Although these are but two examples of the objectification of slaves, it is misleading to regard slaves in the Ottoman Empire as objects. As opposed to "mute property" (*mal-i sâmit*), such as real estate and personal items, they occupied a special position in shariah law as "property-with-voice" (*mal-i-natık*), a position shared with livestock.[4] By necessity, these categories provide a static definition of status, which does not do justice to the role of slaves within a local community. Not only were slaves vital to the expansion of empire but, as part of a society based on social and spatial mobility, their status was also dynamic.[5]

In the early decades of the sixteenth century, when the empire and its institutions were still undergoing transition, slavery was an integral part of that transition. Labor was imperative for fueling the expanding empire and, where a subject population was insufficient in number, subjects were created out of slaves. Upon manumission or completion of their contracts, former slaves entered the subject *reaya* class or, more rarely, the ruling military *askerî* class, the latter path theoretically not open to subjects. There, they blended into an already heterogeneous society where they bought property, married, engaged in commerce, and purchased their own slaves, further adding to the mix of empire. While enslaved, they used the law courts along with, and sometimes against, Muslim and non-Muslim subjects and members of the *askerî* class. In short, during their period of transition they were neither subject nor object.

The records of the imperial city suggest that, with regard to slavery, the concept of stasis may be better replaced with liminality.[6] The anthropologist Victor Turner suggests that liminality occurs during periods of transition "when the past has lost its grip and the future has not yet taken definite shape."[7] One of the protocols of legitimacy requires that a ruler bring order to society, and to its laws, which he reinforces through acts of ritual. Ritualization, a key component of legitimation, was characteristic of the early years of the reign of Süleyman Kanunî (1520–66), especially within the inner confines of the palace and in the inculcation of its slaves.[8] Turner has outlined three stages in the rites of passage or transition, which may be reasonably applied to the institution of slavery: separation of the initiates from everyday life; instruction by practice and precept in a secluded, "marginal," or "liminal" place; and reincorporation into the quotidian community. Although the concept of liminality may be more closely applied to the *devşirme* (conscription of *reaya* children into *askerî* class) and imperial slave households, it is an intriguing idea to consider within the context of the domestic and commercial slavery prevalent in the local communities. It is especially relevant when we consider that the relationship of sultan to subject was extended through practice and precept to master and slave.[9]

In the following, Turner's three stages are used to examine the transition of this "property with voice" into the community. Emphasis is on the second, or liminal, stage in which the slave receives instruction by precept and practice. The legal system is central to this stage, both in supporting the often-contracted responsibilities of master and slave to each other and in providing a venue for transition of the slave from "property with voice" to freedman. In addition, the courts provided the link between the Sublime Porte and society.

The law registers of this time provide an incomparable record of daily life and provide unique insight into the institution of slavery: they record the actions of slaves within an everyday context.

The court records of Üsküdar, a suburb on the Asian shore of Istanbul, are the earliest series for the imperial city and thus provide a base for study of later periods.[10] Furthermore, because they are not yet as systematized as the court records would become under Süleyman and his *şeyhülislâm* (chief Muslim juriconsult), Ebussuüd Efendi, the intermixture of cases provides a rich cross-section of society across class, religion, gender, and occupation.

At the beginning of the sixteenth century, when the community of Üsküdar was about to reap the rewards of an expanding empire, the town, like its residents, was in transition. Approximately fifteen percent of its estimated population of 30,000 residents were non-Muslim and conversion was common. Greek, Armenian, Turkish, Farsi, Kurdish, Slavic, and Central Asian dialects were all languages of the hans, caravansaries, and artisans' quarters. At the beginning of Süleyman's reign, women of the imperial household had already begun to endow charitable foundations, hospices, and soup kitchens to tend the itinerant or poor, among whom the residents of a local leprosarium received special attention.[11] Over the following decades the social architecture would be changed by hunting palaces and kiosks of the sultan and his consorts, and with dervish lodges and mosques that would later establish the town as a center of religious learning.

1. Separation of Initiates

The first stage of inculcation into the new society involved severing the past, a process that was not always successful.[12] Slaves began their passage into local communities through capture during either military campaigns or commercial slave raids. Records of fugitive slaves in the local community during the 1520s confirm that Ottoman campaigns into the Balkans and Crimean raids into Russia and Poland were the primary points of capture for slaves and indicate that the regional mix of the palace was also representative of society in general. According to these court records, the origins of captured slaves were Russian (*Rusî*; some designated as *Moskovî*), thirty-nine percent; Croatian (*Hırvadî*), thirty-one percent; and Bosnian (*Bosnevî*), eleven percent. The remainder was distributed among Hungarian (*Macarî*), Wallachian (*Eflâk*), and Bulgarian (*Bulgarî*) origins.[13] Although there were fluctuations in the mix according to the specific campaign (the number of Hungarians, for example, rose towards the end of the decade), slaves of African (referred to as "*siyah*"/black, *Arab*, or *Habeş*/Abyssinian),[14] Circassian (*Çerkes*), Albanian (*Arnavut*), and Greek (*Rumî*) origin were rare, as were Italian or other Europeans (*Firengî*), who were generally more costly.

During the reign of Süleyman, attempts were made to restrict the sale of slaves to the markets of Istanbul proper,[15] but in the first decade of his reign slaves still made their entry directly into the local community of Üsküdar through markets in the surrounding towns and villages.[16] They also entered the community through more indirect channels: fugitive slaves were sold or auctioned by the *beytülmal* (public treasury) if, after their 100-day holding period had expired, they remained unclaimed.[17] Because of their proven unreliability and tendency to flee, these unclaimed fugitive slaves were often sold at a reduced price and returned if unsatisfactory. At the end of Rebiyülâhır 934 (mid-January 1528), for example, Hacı Halil b. İvas appeared in court (6.21a), and gave the simple statement, "I bought a fugitive slave from the *emin*, Timurhan. I now return him." No reason was given, and no questions were asked.

Under Süleyman's reign, ownership of slaves by non-Muslims (*zimmis*) became theoretically restricted; however, court records of Üsküdar in this first decade indicate that slave ownership crossed the lines of religion and ethnicity. On 26 September 1529, for example, the Greek Dimitri purchased two fugitive slaves at auction (6:155b), whereas exactly six years earlier, Yorgi b. Dimitri and Todora b. Mihal, residents of the rural village of Tellak Ova, claimed three fugitive slaves (3:127b–128a) who had been captured together and brought to court. Neither was this restriction effective after the death of Süleyman.[18] The same *defter* (register) above for Istanbul in 1612 includes a manumission statement that shows that both the slave owners and the slave were non-Muslim (1.1.15). In it, the *zimmi* Andorya Papa Manol and his wife, Korista bint Yani, freed the female slave Istamata bint Dimitri. In this example, conversion to Islam was not a requirement for manumission.

Ideally, when a slave was purchased he or she was considered a member of the master's extended household, over whom the master served as guardian. In this arrangement the slave was re-created during the final passage of manumission discussed below, a process akin to creating a son, or an extension of the self.[19] According to Qur'anic ideal, masters were instructed to provide slaves with adequate lodging and payment for their services.[20] Provision of clothing was also an important symbolic act of identity formation as well as a practical requirement. Records of fugitives confirm that clothing worn by slaves was not unlike that of the Ottoman-at-large, and that it conformed to that worn by the master in appearance and status. In a society where clothing and outward appearance were regulated as symbols of position and rank, the sartorial relationship between slave and master may be considered an extension of their social and legal relationship.

In practice, another less subjective variation was instituted. Skilled slaves were entered into work contracts with their masters where they would be manumitted upon completion of certain terms, either a specific number of years or a quota of goods or services to be completed.[21] The court cases in which slaves most often appear after the death of their masters, as discussed below, involve renegotiation or recognition of the terms of contract originally set by the deceased. Even in this initial state of transition, the property is considered to have legal voice and to be able to engage in a contractual relationship.

2. Instruction by Practice and Precept

Inculcation by practice is readily observable in the town of Üsküdar and the surrounding villages. Agricultural slaves were employed by farmers and local Greek subjects, harvested the market gardens, grain fields, orchards, and old Byzantine vineyards, and manned the fisheries and yogurt houses, which supplied the palace.[22] Slaves herded sheep (6:9b, 72a, 159a), made specialized pastries in bakeries (6.26a, 51b), combed and beat cotton essential for mattresses and cushions (6.99a), and worked as oarsmen (3.16b). Day laborers and slaves worked the docks loading and unloading small boats and skiffs that shuttled provisions and passengers across and along the shores. In the Square of the Falconers that served as rendezvous point for military campaigns and the pilgrimage to Mecca as well as a market place, servants ran errands for their households. In the private households of middle-class Üsküdar, they served as less-glorified domestic servants and wet-nurses (3.76a), rather than the fancified position of rich man's odalisque.[23] Skilled slaves became factotums for their masters, often representing them in commerce and trade (6.32a). During their servitude slaves were paid for their labor on a level that was slightly less than day laborers.

Apprenticeship was one path of integration into a community; marriage offered another. The records suggest that marriage between slave and non-slave was legally recognized if not socially accepted. The Muslim woman Fatma bint Mahmut, for example, sought a divorce from her husband Ferhad b. Abdullah, a manumitted slave and convert, and in so doing ceded her dowry (6:51a). The records also indicate that slaves who were still under contract could marry free women, including Muslims, and that marriage between free man and slave woman also occurred. When Yusuf b. Abdullah, the contracted slave of Musa the cabinet-maker, required personal surety or bond, his Muslim wife, Salcuk bint Mustafa, provided it for him.[24] In yet another case, the Muslim male Mehmet b. Çalabverdi appeared in court to claim the freedom of a female slave to whom he was engaged (6:135a). When her mistress, Fatma bint Ahmet, had died, her heirs refused to acknowledge the slave's claim that she had been freed upon Fatma's death. Mehmet claims that upon betrothal he had given the young bride several gifts, including household furnishings. The engagement, although agreed upon and registered by the slave's mistress, was denied by the heirs and her representative.

Whereas practice served to integrate slaves into a local community through the labor force, it also instated them as extensions of master and household. Through practice, the normative values of Islam and empire were instilled. It is through legal precept, however, and the access to and use of Islamic law that the slave began to cross the boundary between original and future status, from infidel slave to Muslim Ottoman subject.

As an intermediary between sultan and subject, the shariah court intervened in the regulation of slavery, and although later than the period under study, a judicial decree to the residents of Istanbul is still relevant here. One of the first entries in the new registers of Istanbul created in 1021 (1612) was an order regarding the manumission of slaves (1.1.1a). According to an imperial edict, all slaves of the Jewish and Christian (*kâfir*) communities (*taife*), that is, who were non-Muslim in origin, and manumitted during the previous six years, had to secure a new proof from the *sicill* (judicial record). Furthermore, the action was to be undertaken within three days in all quarters of the city. Subsequently, there was a unprecedented number of manumissions recorded at this time (approximately 60, evenly divided between male and female).

The *Kanun-name* (code of laws) of Selim I specifies that slaves did not receive the same punishment as that given to residents or subjects. Indeed, in cases of assault, for example, slaves were issued half the punishment of free subjects.[25] Furthermore, a *fetva* (juridical opinion) issued by Ebussuüd Efendi underlined the responsibility of the master for the slave's actions: "If Zeyd's slaves go a-whoring, drink wine, fight, throw stones at the neighbors' houses and break windows, and if Zeyd knows about these actions and remains silent, what does the law say in this respect?"[26] The reply was that Zeyd, too, should be punished and jailed, as should the slaves. During this period of transition, the master is clearly responsible for his charge.

The intermediary role of the court in the protection and safekeeping of property entrusted to it is clear, even if that property is a captured fugitive slave, and especially when the plaintiff is a member of the *ulema*. In an extended case (6.13b), Yunus Fakîh bin Ramazan, the substitute judge from the town of İznikmid, claimed: "I own a Bosnian slave. He ran away." Yunus Fakîh addressed İskender bin Abdullah, the assistant to the *subası* (superintendent) of Orhonlu. "When he was in your jail, he escaped." İskender acknowledged that it was he who had captured and jailed the slave, and from whom the slave had also escaped in Rebiyülevvel 934 (November 1529). Mevlana Yunus's complaint was a financial one: the slave still had four years on his contract for which he had not been compensated "one *pare* from the village" (6.14a). Soon after, a compromise was registered in which he accepted 600 akçe in reparations (6.18b).

Use of the court by slaves shares many traits with that by members of the community-at-large, but there appears to be a clear distinction. In general, free members of the subject and ruling classes, Muslim and non-Muslim, male and female, appear to have used the courts as a last resort, either when a dispute could not be resolved within the family or other parties involved or when notarization of a transaction was required. The records of slave use of the shariah court suggests that the opposite was true for slaves, who used it as a place in which to legitimate their status vis-à-vis the community. That is, before they were incorporated into a community and established social links within it, slaves relied upon the law to uphold and protect their rights of transition.

The distinction between "property with voice" and "mute property" is apparent if we examine the use of the shariah courts by slaves. Often upon death of their masters, slaves turned to the court to contest heirs who had tried to deny the conditions expressed by the deceased, either freedom upon the master's death, or renegotiated terms of contract. Heirs often tried to sell contracted slaves at full price, disregarding the length of term already served. Following the death of the wealthy Gülamşah (6.30) at the end of Cemaziyelâhır 934 (mid-March, 1528), for example, the female slave Nevşire and the male slave Kasım were put up for sale. They claimed, however, to have been freed. The court investigated and registered the opinion that they had 6 months remaining of their contracts.

As mentioned above, it was not uncommon for a slave to reassert the terms of manumission upon the death of his master. When the farmer Yunus bin Mustafa died in January 1529, one of his two agricultural slaves, Hamza, had only two years remaining on his contract (6:72a). He claimed in court that before Yunus' death arrangements had been made (*takdir olup*) for the time remaining to be reduced to only one year. His claim was investigated and verified.[27] The relationship in court of slave to master (or former master) was not always antagonistic and, in some cases, was indicative of the social and familial bond established between them. When, for example, in 1528 Ali b. Mahmut, a resident of the Herekle quarter of Üsküdar, registered a unspecified complaint against Ferhad b. Abdullah, the slave of Katib Hişam Bey, the slave's master provided personal surety for him (6.29b).

It is clear, then, that although slaves may have held the legal status of property, they had access to the courts and used them to contest the estate of the deceased. The actions of the slave Gülbahar bint Abdullah indicate that female slaves also used the courts to uphold their contracts of manumission. Gülbahar addressed Ayşe Hatun bint Sanduk in court and stated that when the time of manumission came due, her mistress had denied the contract and instead tried to sell her (6:128b). In her statement of response, it is clear that Gülbahar was aware of her terms of contract and placed her faith in the legal system to uphold them: she astutely questions how she, a Muslim convert, could be enslaved after manumission.

The practice of pro-rating the contract of a slave appears common, and in these we also hear the voice of the property in dispute. At the end of July 1519 (Receb 925) [Marula] bint Süleyman wife of Said bin Durmuş came to the court arguing that when Küseç Bali's master had died, the slave still had 8 years of service left on his contract (1.98). An agreement was reached that 100 akçe would be taken for each year remaining. By comparison, in mid-March 928, an unnamed slave with two and a half years on contract was sold for 1,105 akçe (6.31a). This compromise action is similar to that in the sale of Yunus Fakîh's slave, above.

In these cases, it is clear that the status of the slave is that of property. Slave status, however, did not exempt a slave from ultimate responsibility for his or her actions although, as noted above, slaves received a less severe punishment for their crimes. One noteworthy case involved the slave Kadem bint Abdullah, who was accused of stealing the sizable amount of 4,000 akçe from İbrahim b. Kemal Beğ of Gece quarter (6.27a). When she was summoned to court in March 1528, she acknowledged taking the money, but added that she had given it to the convert Ahmet bin Abdullah, who was also summoned. Other than the personal surety given for Ahmet, the resolution was not recorded.

Slaves were also called to testify against each other. The servant of Hoca Abdullah b. İsa was summoned to testify against another who was accused of stealing a piece of embroidery (6.6b). Slave owners took their slaves to court on equally mundane matters. An entry in which a woman placed a claim against her female slave for ruining the laundry is also indicative of how women used the court to solve everyday problems (3.76a). In it the *kadı* (judge) decided that the slave had to pay her mistress Gümüş Hatun one hundred akçe, an amount representing several months' pay, in compensation for the fine piece of gauze that had been destroyed during its laundering. The slave was responsible for the cloth, used as a head cloth or face veil, even though she claimed she had given it to someone else to handle.

3. Reincorporation into the Quotidian Community

As Halil İnalcık has clearly demonstrated in a study of fifteenth-century Bursa, slaves and manumitted slaves (*atîk*) "formed an energetic, enterprising class in society."[28] Moreover, since both slave and freedman were found in both the highest ranks and broadest range of society, their status was not considered derogatory. By definition, example had already been set by the sultans, themselves the progeny of slave mothers.

In an empire that prided itself on meritocracy, slavery was a path to advancement as well as a passage from ignorance to enlightenment.[29] The manumission of slaves, encouraged by Islam as a praiseworthy act, entered the slave directly into the subject class (6.10b), and, if the slave converted, into the Muslim *ümmet* (community). Although a slave could be considered the equal of the former master with regard to social transactions, the legal relationship was that of progeny rather than co-equals. The familial bond between slave and master continued after manumission, often with the former slave taking on the status of "client" and continuing in the service of the family. According to Halil Sahillioğlu, former masters oversaw the final transition of freedmen into the Ottoman community.[30]

Among the manumitted slaves of note in Üsküdar was the wealthy Gülfem Hatun. An *atîk* of the sultan, she established a foundation in March 1543 for the construction of a timber-frame mosque in a downtown quarter that would continue to bear her name.[31] Several estates, however, indicate that the lives of freedmen and women were remarkable only for the ordinariness of their possessions and social transaction recorded at the time of death. Their estates are indistinguishable from those of other residents, such as the estate of Paşabeği bint Hoşkadem, the manumitted slave of İsa bin Yusuf (3.25b). Although an estate captures social and financial interactions at one specific time in a person's life—the time of an individual's death—it is clear that Paşabeği was both socially and financially integrated. She left behind a series of sizable credit transactions undertaken with men not related to her from the village, transactions which were typical of those undertaken by members of the community across lines of gender and religion. Her possessions included a small house that she owned in the rural village of Bulgurlu, some livestock, and an orchard, the kind of property commonly found in the possession of other women of the town.

The appearances of *atîk* in court were as mundane as other subjects. A manumitted slave who worked as an oarsman, for example, was featured in a case in which the *mültezim* or tax-farmer for the boatmen of Üsküdar brought a claim against his former master (3.16b). The case of Gümüş Hatun, likely a freedwoman herself, taking her own slave to court over the laundry has already been mentioned. In another incident, the wife of a manumitted slave is accused of beating a *hacı* who had entered her house (6.3.44b–45a). Her husband was a resident of Üsküdar, but she apparently maintained a rented house in Istanbul. Countercharges were leveled against the *hacı* and his companion. Here, the husband, a freedman, was held responsible for the wife's actions, just as his former master had previously been responsible for him.[32]

The legal relationship of slave to master that continued after manumission is also indicated in the local records. Indeed, as this relationship continued after death through the heir-by-derived-relationship (*asabe-i sebebiye*), former masters, or their heirs, were entitled under certain circumstances to a share of their former slaves' estate.[33] Their claim replaced that of the state or the *beytülmal*. For example, when the freedwoman Fatma Hatun bint Abdullah died in the house of Hoca Mehmet bin Salih in March 1530, her estate was inherited by Mehmet's wife, Fatma bint Yunus, her former mistress (6.127a). Fatma's modest estate of 354 akçe consisted of worn clothing, flax thread, and hand-worked textiles typical of the estates of many women: an embroidered velvet cushion cover, bed covers, and an old hand-worked waist sash.

In that the relationship to her master continued after death, the voice, if not the will, of Paşabeği shows that she resorted to a legal strategy to retain the last word. Like many women who sought to control the distribution of their estates, she willed the maximum amount of the one-third permitted by law, and thus was able to partly regulate its distribution after her death. Masters also made claims upon the estates of their slaves who had not been emancipated. When the Georgian slave Beşaret b. Abdullah died, his master Ali Beğ bin Mansur Beğ claimed 850 akçe from his former slave's estate. The conditions of indebtedness, whether a loan or the incompletion of a work contract, unfortunately are not mentioned.

The estate of İskender b. Abdullah, *atîk* of Captain (Reis) Davud Beğ, indicates that freed slaves could also share in the local prosperity of the expanding empire (6.32a). İskender's estate entry is brief, but informative. We can ascertain from the title of his former master, a sea captain, and by the commercial quarter of the town in which he died, as well as the high value of his estate (6,000 akçe), that İskender, like his master, was involved in commerce. Moreover, İskender had taken a loan with interest from a foundation overseen by the Bozacı Şirmerd b. Abdullah, on which 300 akçe was still outstanding. İskender, like the farmer Hasan, below, appears to have continued to work in the field into which his master had brought him, but in commerce rather than agriculture.

The community court records confirm that freedmen also owned their own slaves, thereby perpetuating the institution which originally had brought them into the local community. Hasan bin Abdullah, the *atîk* of the landowner Süleyman, died in the rural village of Reislu in mid-November 1527, after the winter crops of wheat, fodder, and flax had been sown (6.9b). His estate is indistinguishable from estates of other farmers, except that the total evaluation was higher than that of his peers.

Examination of his effects shows that his existence was one of hardship but enterprise. He lived in a meager house evaluated at 200 akçe and described as little more than a shed with attached quarters for his work animals. Against this, his estate showed that he was heavily in debt and also that his most valuable investment had been the purchase of his own slave, İlyas. The slave was valued at 1,800 akçe.[34] After a dispute was settled between Süleyman's heirs (the master had predeceased his slave), İlyas was passed on to the son of the former master. The familial relationship of master to slave was thus legally transferred to the son of the master and the slave of the master's freedman.

Conclusions

It is clear from the court cases above that during their period of transition from slavery to freedom, slaves were not separated from the resident community. On the contrary, they began their incorporation by participating in it, working alongside freedmen and subjects. In this period of liminality, however, the role of the courts was especially important in enforcing the new identity and the rights associated with this transitional status of property, yet with legal voice. Unlike residents who were able to resort to the established networks of family, quarter, or community to reach a compromise on a dispute, slaves resorted to the letter of the law to reinforce their transitional status and contracts.

Records from estates and capture of fugitives show that the social status and identity of a slave was closely associated with that of his or her master. Slaves, we find, not only took on the familial identity, professions, and communities of their masters, but during the process of transition took on the intimate identity of the individual through the clothing of their patrons. The proprietary relationship established between master and slave continued legally and socially after the slave was incorporated into the community. This relationship was further perpetuated by freedmen who purchased their own slaves whose incorporation they would oversee. When slaves became converts as well as subjects their new status was marked by a renaming: son or daughter of Abdullah, slave of God. Little else now distinguished them from their fellow residents.

Notes

based on research undertaken in Müftülük Archives of ... s generously funded by a grant from the Fulbright-Hays ... American Research Institute in Turkey. The assistance of Dr. Abdülaziz Bayındır, Director of the Archives, is greatly appreciated.

1. The core resources used are from the Üsküdar series of shariah court records, which are the earliest series available for the city: İstanbul Şeri Sicilleri: Üsküdar Series 6, volumes 1–7 (abbreviated by volume and recto or verso page number, 2:98a, or 7:21b, for example). Records from the court districts of Galata and Istanbul are indicated when used (series 4, and series 1 and 5, respectively).
2. The reverse is found where Karhaman, a female slave, is recorded among the household utensils, next to a coffee pot, but before the contents of the stable. Many more of these examples, where the slave is treated as an object among the property of the deceased, exist in the court registers. See, for example, Üsküdar 6:193.25b; Istanbul 5:1.106a, 122b, and 2.121a; and Galata 14.2.38b–39a, 14.4.11, and 14.8.2.
3. The correlation between the value of slaves and residences was observed by Sahillioğlu in connection with Bursa also at the beginning of the sixteenth century (1985: 95). To achieve a relative value for the akçe at this time, the *nafaka* or court-appointed allotment of 2 akçe for daily subsistence to widows and divorced women is useful. This amount roughly correlated with retirement pay for mosque assistants as well as the wages of day laborers. See Seng, 1996: 154.
4. Sahillioğlu, 1985: 50. Although Paul Forand (1971: 59–66) refers to the "slave's condition of being in the category of either domestic animals or inanimate objects," the shariah's differentiation is quite clear: slaves are in the category of the former, not the latter.
5. Regarding the recognized symbolism of slavery, Forand states that according to al-Bukhari, slaves belonged in the category of the dead. I quote from his translation: ". . . freedom is the attribute par excellence of a living being in secular jurisdiction, whereas slaves are in the category of the dead, for servitude is a vestige of obstinacy in refusing to believe in the One God (*kufr*)—and this in the eyes of the law is death itself …." (1971: 61).
6. Turner, 1982: 25.
7. Meyerhof, 1982: 116.
8. Necipoğlu, 1991: 3–30.

9. Kunt, 1983: passim.

10. Centered on the town itself in which the *kadı* presided, the *kaza* or legal district formed a crescent about twelve miles wide that stretched from the Black Sea to the Bay of İzmit, approximately two days' horse ride in each direction.

11. Lepers were another group who were considered by law to be in transition, in this case, between the living and the dead. Unlike their European counterparts who had no legal rights or protection, however, lepers in the imperial city were considered to hold a special position as intercessors. They therefore maintained a legal status and a functioning role within society. Their lodge abutted the extensive cemetery of Karaca Ahmet, where for a fee dropped into a bowl carved into a rock, they recited verses of the Qu'ran and said prayers for the dead. See Seng, 1991, chapter 1.

12. As seen in Leslie Peirce's provocative work on the imperial harem in the seventeenth century, the articulation of origin was expressed in the factions of the palace (1996; passim). These ties to ethnic and regional origins are also expressed in the chronicles of the sixteenth-century historian Mustafa Ali (Fleischer, 1986: passim), and in Metin Kunt's aforementioned work on the palace slave system.

13. Seng, 1996: 157.

14. For clarification of terms, see Ronald Jennings' extensive footnotes (1987: 286–302).

15. Mantran, 1986: 2; 106–108.

16. For example, a slave market was held in July 1521 in İstavros, a village just north of Üsküdar (3.2a). The noise made at the public auction disturbed the villagers so much that they took their protest to court.

17. The incidence of slave escapes is not conclusive evidence that slaves ran away in order to return to their home villages. Court records indicate that although some of these slaves had fled long distances in an attempt at freedom, others used the strategy of flight in order to be resold into another household.

18. According to Mantran (1986: 2; 112–13), by the end of the seventeenth century the practice of slave ownership by non-Muslims was legalized. Instead of the legal gyration of having Muslim intermediaries purchase slaves for them, non-Muslims were taxed for the slaves owned.

19. See Forand, 1971: 60–61. For a discussion of the implications of manumission in Islamic law, see Shaun Marmon, "Domestic Slavery in the Mamluk Empire: A Preliminary Sketch," in this volume. For a discussion of liminal-

ity and the relationship between sufi master and disciple see Malamud, 64, no. 1: 89–117.

20. According to Suraiya Faroqhi, the payment for services was at or below subsistence level. The subsistence allowance for an adult male slave at the end of the sixteenth century was 2–3 akçe per day, less than 1 akçe for a young servant girl, and 1 akçe for a boy household servant. An alternative arrangement also included a suit of clothing, similar to the master's or in keeping with his status, and 400 akçe in cash (1984: 279). Persons engaged in menial occupations received a subsistence allowance of 2 akçe per day at this time. This amount was also assigned for the upkeep of incarcerated slaves, stray livestock, and as the daily allowance of divorced women during their three-month waiting period. In Bursa at the end of the fifteen century, the living expenses for a female slave were estimated at 40 akçe per month (Halil İnalcık, 1979: 44).

21. For the use of slaves in the production of Bursa silk, for example, see İnalcık, 1979: 27–31. Barkan gives examples of financially successful manumitted slaves who purchase their own slaves (1966: 24–30).

22. Seng, 1996: 136–37.

23. The observations of Oghier Ghiselin de Busbecq (Forster and Daniell, 1968: 209–11) and Hans Dernschwam (1987: passim) are pertinent here. See also Seng (1998: passim).

24. Personal surety (*kefil bi'l-nefs*) or bond as set for Yusuf was required for artisans and workmen to ensure responsibility for their actions and indicates that he may have been a skilled artisan working for the cabinetmaker. Muslims and non-Muslims provided bond for each other across lines of religion and ethnicity. Although fewer cases exist, women also provided bond for their husbands, as did the non-Muslim wife of a Greek tavern owner.

25. Pulaha, 1987: parts 1 and 2; 52–53.

26. Düzdağ, Fetva no. 542; 1983: 120.

27. See also 6:99a, 6:26a, 6.51b, and 52a–b.

28. İnalcık, 1993: 183.

29. Fisher, 1980: 49–56.

30. Sahillioğlu, 1985: 60.

31. These registers are housed in Başbakanlık Archives and referred to in Konyalı, 1976: 1; 46–47.

32. According to the *Kanun-name*, husbands were also held responsible for the behavior of their wives, and for the fines and punishments involved.

33. The "derived relationship" or *asabe-i sebebiye* differed from the extended or collateral blood relationship or *binefsihi*. In the case of the spouse of the *i'tak* being the only heir, if there were no offspring, the spouse received only one-fourth of the estate. The remainder went to the past master. Sahillioğlu describes emancipation as "[giving] birth to a new type of client relationship, replacing that of bondage" (1985: 60–61). See also Barkan for a description of these relationships in fourteenth-century Ottoman Edirne (1966: 24–30).

34. If we use the rate of 2 akçe per day for a field laborer's wage, Hasan had invested the disproportionate amount of almost three years' wages to acquire him.

References

Barkan, Ömer Lûtfi. "Edirne 'Askeri Kassımı'na Âit Tereke Defterleri (1545–1659)." *Belgeler* 3, nos. 5–6 (1966): 1–497.

Brunschvig, R. "ʿAbd." *Encyclopedia of Islam*. 2d ed. Leiden: E.J. Brill, 1960. 1:24–40.

Dernschwam, Hans. *İstanbul ve Anadolu'ya Seyahat Günlüğü*. Translated by Yaşar Önen. Ankara: Kültür ve Türizm Bakanlığı, 1987.

Düzdağ, M. Ertuğrul. *Şeyhülislâm Ebussuüd Efendi Fetvaları*. İstanbul: Enderun Kitabevi, 1983.

Faroqhi, Suraiya. *Towns and Townsmen of Ottoman Anatolia: Trade, Crafts, and Food Production in an Urban Setting*. London / New York: Cambridge University Press, 1984.

Fisher, A. "Studies in Ottoman Slavery and Slave Trade, II: Manumission." *Journal of Turkish Studies* 4 (1980): 49–56.

Fleischer, Cornell H. *Bureaucrat and Intellectual in the Ottoman Empire: The Historian Mustafa Ali (1541–1600)*. Princeton, N.J.: Princeton University Press, 1986.

Forand, Paul. "The Relation of the Slave and the Client to the Master or Patron in Medieval Islam," *International Journal of Middle East Studies* 2 (1971): 59–66.

Forster, Charles Thorton, and F. H. Blackburne Daniell, translators. *The Turkish Letters of Ogier Ghiselin de Busbecq*. 2 vols. Oxford: Clarendon Press, 1968.

İnalcık, Halil. "Servile Labor in the Ottoman Empire," in *The Mutual Effects of the Islamic and Judaeo-Christian Worlds: The Eastern European Pattern*. Edited by Abraham Ascher, Tibor Halasi-Kuhn, and Bela K. Kiraly, 22–52.

New York: Columbia University Press, 1979.

Jennings, Ronald. "Black Slaves and Free Slaves in Ottoman Cyprus, 1590–1640," *Journal of Economic and Social History of the Orient* 30, No. 3 (1987): 286–302.

Konyalı, İbrahim Hakkî. *Âbideleri ve Kitabeleriyle Üsküdar Tarihi*. İstanbul: Türkiye Yeşilay Yayınevi, 1976.

Kunt, Metin. *The Sultan's Servants: The Transformation of Ottoman Provincial Government, 1550–1650*. New York: Columbia University Press, 1983.

Malamud, Margaret. "Gender and Spiritual Self-Fashioning: The Master-Disciple Relationship in Classical Sufism." *Journal of the American Academy of Religion* 64, no. 1: 89–117.

Mantran, Robert. *17. Yüzyıl İkinci Yarısında İstanbul*. 2 vols. Ankara: Verso Yayınları, 1986.

Necipoğlu, Gülrü. *Architecture, Ceremonial and Power: The Topkapı Palace in the Fifteenth and Sixteenth Centuries*. Boston: MIT Press, 1991.

Peirce, Leslie. *The Imperial Harem: Women and Sovereignty in the Ottoman Empire*. Oxford: Oxford University Press, 1993.

Pulaha, Selami, and Yaşar Yücel. "Le Code (Kānūnnāme) de Selim Ier (1512–1520) et Certaines Autres Lois de la Deuxième Moitié du XVIe Siècle." *Belgeler* 12, No. 16 (1987): 1–100.

Sahillioğlu, Halil. "Slaves in the Social and Economic Life of Bursa in the Late 15th and Early 16th Centuries." *Turcica* 17 (1985): 7–42.

Seng, Yvonne J. "Fugitives and Factotums: Slaves in Early Sixteenth-Century Istanbul." *Journal of Economic and Social History of the Orient* 39, No. 2 (1996): 136–67.

Seng, Yvonne J. "The Üsküdar Tereke as Records of Everyday Life in an Ottoman Town, 1521–1524." Ph.D. diss., University of Chicago, 1991.

Turner, Victor, ed. *Celebration: Studies in Fertility and Ritual*. Washington, D.C.: Smithsonian Institution Press, 1982.

Islamic Law and Polemics over Race and Slavery in North and West Africa (16th–19th Century)

JOHN HUNWICK

Introduction

In his book *Race and Slavery in Islam*, Bernard Lewis makes the double point that although Muslims of the Middle East never practiced the kind of racial discrimination and oppression that persons of European descent practiced in apartheid South Africa, and "until recently in the United States," Muslim societies were never idyllic havens of "racial innocence."[1] In a general sense both propositions are valid. Indeed, one might hardly expect that Muslims would be uniquely free of racial stereotyping and ingrained prejudices, either about black Africans or any other human group. In the Muslim world, attitudes towards various human groups have been most obviously an artifact of the single great prejudice of Muslim peoples—the prejudice against "unbelievers," for these were the archetypal "other."[2] They were also the enslaveable other. Hence being a slave marked one as an unbeliever, or at any rate a former unbeliever, for slavery was both a result of unbelief and, in most cases, a cure for it.[3] Black Africans were the single fairly clearly identifiable group whose presence in Mediterranean Muslim society was largely attributable to slavery, and thus to former unbelief. Racial prejudice there thus has within it an undercurrent of religious coloration.

Once the black slave had been manumitted, he or she was received into the community of the faithful and shared, at least in legal theory, in both the privileges and the duties of other believers of whatever color or race.[4] If the law was clear on such matters, was public opinion always as enlightened? The answer to this question can only be discovered in social histories of individual Muslim communities. The present essay, while in no sense an essay in social history, attempts to look at debates that took place in both West and North Africa from the sixteenth to the late nineteenth century about the relationship between blackness of skin and slavery. What we see is a clear tension between the idealism of the *sharīʿa* and certain attitudes—no doubt of long standing—about black Africans. In Morocco these attitudes emanated from the ruling class, and either reflected or influenced popular opinion, so that a late-nineteenth-century writer could claim that "many common folk believe that the reason for being enslaved according to the Holy Law is merely that a man should be black in color and come from those regions [sc. *bilād al-sūdān*]."[5]

Legal theory

The argument about who might be owned as a slave was an old one in northern Africa, especially since that region's principal source of slaves was in far distant West Africa, where by the sixteenth century conversion to Islam had been an ongoing process for seven centuries. From the point of view of the jurists there were two principles: first, that the innate condition of people is freedom (*al-aṣl huwa 'l-ḥurriyya*), and that there is thus a presumption of freedom in the absence of compelling proof to the contrary; second, that only the unbeliever who has refused the summons to place himself under Muslim governance (either by converting to Islam or, in the case of "Scriptuaries" (*ahl al-kitāb*) and certain other groups assimilated to them, paying the poll-tax) may be enslaved after having been defeated in a lawfully constituted *jihād*.[6] The condition for a lawfully constituted *jihād* was that it be conducted by the caliph as *amīr al-muʾminīn* or his duly appointed regional governor. Such a *jihād* should have as its object "the elevation of the word of God" (*iʿlāʾ kalimat Allāh*), i.e. the furtherance of the cause of Islam through the establishment of governance under the *sharīʿa*.

Although objective conditions in the African Muslim world made it difficult if not impossible for such conditions to be fulfilled, the jurists continued to hold to them. Even before the destruction of the ʿAbbāsid caliphate of Baghdad in 1258, few rulers sought confirmation of their rule from any caliph. Even fewer did so during the period of what might be called the "mock caliphate" in Mamlūk Egypt from 1260 to 1517. Askiya *al-ḥājj* Muḥammad of Songhay, who met the ʿAbbāsid caliph al-Mustamsik in Cairo in 1498 and obtained delegated authority from him,[7] was one of the few to do so. From the strictly legal point of view, then, the vast majority of wars waged by Muslims against non-Muslims in West Africa down to this period could not be considered *jihād*s, and hence the enslavement of persons captured could not be considered lawful. In point of fact, the caliphal title *amīr al-muʾminīn* was used after 1258 by certain North and West African rulers, although generally they did not thereby presume to make a claim on the caliphate in the historic sense of that institution. However, the Saʿdian and ʿAlawid rulers of Morocco (who claimed sharīfian and thus Quraysh ancestry) saw themselves, and encouraged others to see them, as legitimate Muslim rulers ordained by God to rule over the Muslims of western Africa and to initiate *jihād*, and invoked caliphal authority. When, for example, Mai Idrīs Aloma of Bornu (r. 1569–93) asked the Saʿdian sultan Aḥmad al-Manṣūr for firearms to help him pursue the *jihād* against neighboring pagans, he was told quite clearly that he had no right to pursue *jihād* independently, and could do so only on behalf of the *amīr al-muʾminīn* al-Manṣūr after he had acknowledged his overlordship through signing a document of allegiance (*bayʿa*).[8]

West African Legal Opinions

The earliest known ruling on the matter of slavery is a *fatwā* given by al-Makhlūf al-Balbālī (d. after 940/1533–34), who studied both in Fez and Walāta and subsequently taught in Kano, Katsina, Timbuktu, and Marrakesh.[9] While stressing that the cause for enslavement is unbelief (i.e. being a non-Muslim at the time of capture), he sought to establish a rule of thumb based on ethnic origin for deciding *a priori* who might be Muslims and who not. He defined the Muslims as "the people of Kano, some of Zakzak (Zaria), the people of Katsina, the people of Gobir, and all of Songhay [and] . . . all the Fullān(i)." Persons known to be from these lands or ethnicities, or who make a claim to be so, should be set free.[10] In fact he refers to a ruling by the *qāḍī* of Timbuktu Maḥmūd b. ʿUmar (held office 1498–1548), who required only that slaves should claim to be from such lands in order to be set free, without actually having to prove it. The reason for such rulings was to avoid what was described as the "catastrophe" of enslaving Muslims, since such action imperiled one's salvation. One way in which one imperiled one's soul was by committing the sin of fornication (*zinā*) by taking as a concubine a slave woman who was in fact a free Muslim woman, though of course sexual relations would be lawful if a woman had been lawfully enslaved. ʿAbd al-Raḥmān al-Saʿdī, author of the *Taʾrīkh al-sūdān*, a seventeenth-century chronicle of Timbuktu, who reported on the sexual and other misdeeds of Sunni ʿAlī (ruler of Songhay 1463–92), observed that when this ruler offered some captured Fulani women as concubines to scholars of Timbuktu, his great-great-grandfather, out of religious scruple, had married the woman who was presented to him rather than take her as a concubine.[11]

The religious ethnography of West Africa was later elaborated in greater detail by *Qāḍī* Maḥmūd's great-nephew, the celebrated Timbuktu jurist Aḥmad Bābā (d. 1627), in replies he gave to inquiries from the central Saharan oasis of Tuwāt, and from southern Morocco. His reply to the inquirers from Tuwāt is a complete treatise on slavery and its peculiar relationship to sub-Saharan Africa and blackness of skin, and bears the title *Miʿrāj al-ṣuʿūd ilā nayl ḥukm majlūb al-sūd* (or alternatively *al-Kashf wa 'l-bayān li-ḥukm majlūb al-sūdān*). The request for information came from Tuwāt and was made by a certain Saʿīd b. Ibrāhīm al-Jirārī. He was concerned about some slaves who had been brought there from Bornu, ʿAfnū,[12] Kano, Jūghū (Gao),[13] and Katsina, which were, according to him, lands "whose adherence to Islam is widely acknowledged among us." Could the Tuwātis deal in such slaves or not? He continued:

> For it is known that in accordance with the *sharīʿa* the reason why it is allowed to own [others] is [their] unbelief. Thus, whoever purchases an unbeliever is permitted to own him, but not in the contrary case. Conversion to Islam subsequent to the existence of the aforementioned condition does not have any effect on continued ownership. Were those lands which we mentioned, and others like them of the lands of the Muslims of the Sūdān, conquered and [their people] enslaved in a state of unbelief, while their conversion occurred afterwards—hence there is no harm [in owning them]—or not? One of the *qāḍī*s of the Sūdān reported that the *imām* who conquered them whilst they were unbelievers chose to spare them as slaves, since he had the choice, or because he did not consider the five well-known options, and that they still remain in a state of slavery, and whenever the sultan needs any of them he brings in as many as he wants. Is this true or not?

The fundamental legal question thus turns on whether the lands mentioned were actually conquered by Muslims (in a presumed *jihād*) while their people were still non-Muslims; in such a case one option would have been to enslave them. What is suggested by the questioner here is that this option was taken, but that the people themselves were left where they were to constitute an endless reservoir of slaves which could be drawn upon at will by Muslim rulers. In accordance with Islamic law, subsequent conversion to Islam would not have changed their status as slaves. This would, indeed, be an extraordinary state of affairs, since Islamic law requires that a slave be owned by an individual master who can manumit him or her at his discretion. However, as will be seen in what follows, the notion of the permanent slave status of black Africans was ingrained in North African thinking about them.

A second part to his question concerned slaves whose land of origin was unknown, nor was it known if they had been enslaved prior to conversion to Islam. Could such persons be bought and sold as slaves without further investigation? As if he knew the answer to his question, al-Jirārī continues:

> Or is investigation mandatory, or [at least] preferable? What is to be done if an investigation is undertaken with inconclusive results? What, then, is the law? Should the word of the slave be accepted or not? Does this come under the heading of doubt about the impediment, and is thus to be rejected, as in [the case of] doubt in divorce and manumission?[14] Or does it come under the heading of doubt about the condition, necessitating the previous existence of that which is the subject of the condition, like [the case] of doubt about legal impurity after a state of legal purity has been known . . . .[15]

In a second inquiry al-Jirārī raises the issue of race; specifically he asks for Aḥmad Bābā's help in understanding what is essentially the classic Hamitic myth encapsulated in a report from the Companion Ibn Masʿūd as reported by al-Suyūṭī in his *Azhār al-ʿurūsh fī akhbār al-ḥubūsh*:[16] "Noah bathed and saw his son looking at him, and said to him, 'Are you looking at me whilst I bathe?' [and] God changed his color and he became black, and he is the ancestor of the *sūdān*."[17] Al-Jirārī also cites a statement attributed to al-Ṭabarī: "Noah prayed for Shem that his descendants should be prophets and messengers, and he cursed Ham, praying that his descendants should be slaves to Shem and Japhet," and asks: "What is the meaning of Ham's descendants being slaves to the descendants of Shem and Japhet? If what is meant is the unbelievers among them, then [being slaves] is not restricted to them, nor similarly is [ownership of slaves] restricted to his two brothers Shem and Japhet, since the unbeliever may be owned whether he is black or white." To make his point even more clear in relation to local circumstances, he adds: "What is the significance of restricting slavery through conquest to the *sūdān*, despite the fact that others share with them the quality that necessitates that?" In short, why should black Africans be a unique target of enslavement when any "unbeliever" of any race is equally liable to enslavement from the point of view of the law; similarly why should the slave owning races be the descendants of the other sons of Noah, Shem and Japhet, who are generally identified in medieval Islamic writing as the "ancestors" of the Arabs on the one hand, and of the Turks, Persians, and Slavs on the other?[18]

What al-Jirārī is tacitly alluding to is an underlying presumption that black Africans are inherently deserving of being enslaved by non-black peoples, and that it is necessary to prove that such persons are to be excluded from this presumption by virtue of their being Muslims who converted to Islam without compulsion. As he states clearly: the only condition that renders one liable to enslavement is being a non-Muslim at the time of capture.

Aḥmad Bābā deals with these major questions in his reply written in 1023/1614–15.[19] He asserts that the people of Kano, Katsina, Bornu, and Songhay converted without conquest; indeed, in the case of the latter two, their conversion occurred long ago.[20] He points out, however, that each of these peoples (he essentially means kingdoms) borders on non-Muslim folk whom the Muslims raid, though some of these non-Muslim neighbors apparently have a truce with the Muslims and pay *kharāj*. On the other hand, there are internecine wars, especially between Kano and Katsina, and the resulting captives are sold even if they are Muslims. He is particularly anxious to establish that no *imām* conquered the West African groups he names as Muslims, much less did such an *imām* "prefer to spare them as slaves"; and he questions the report al-Jirārī gives on the authority of "one of the *qāḍī*s of the *sūdān*," challenging him to name the *imām*, and to state what land he conquered and when. He then provides some historical remarks on the Islamization of West Africa, basing himself on Ibn Khaldūn, in order to make his point that the peoples of the region accepted Islam peacefully.[21]

Aḥmad Bābā then turns to the case of those whose land of origin is unknown and whose status is unclear. He comes back to the classic definition of who may be enslaved, and then somewhat enlarges the list of Muslim peoples in his religious ethnography:

> You should be aware that the cause of enslavement is unbelief, and the unbelievers of the *sūdān* are like any other unbelievers in this regard—Jews, Christians, Persians, Berbers, or others whose persistence in unbelief rather than Islam has been established—as will be demonstrated from the words of the *Mudawwana* at the end of this section. This is proof that there is no difference between any unbelievers in this regard.

> Whoever is enslaved in a state of unbelief may rightly be owned, whoever he is, as opposed to those of all groups who converted to Islam first, such as the people of Bornu, Kano, Songhay, Katsina, Gobir, and Mali and some of [the people of] Zakzak.[22] They are free Muslims who may not be enslaved under any circumstance. So also are the majority of the Fullān(i) [Fulbe], except, so we have heard, a group living beyond Jenne who are said to be unbelievers. We do not know if [their unbelief] is ancestral or occurred through apostasy. Indeed, disputes occur between them and they raid one another.

However, this does not answer the question posed to him. He therefore turns to the opinions of jurists of former times and quotes from the *Nawāzil* of the eleventh century Mālikī jurist Ibn Sahl,[23] who cites opinions of Andalusian jurists of the ninth and tenth centuries. With one exception these place the onus of proof on the slave owner, a view that was followed by Makhlūf al-Balbālī and the *qāḍī* of Timbuktu Maḥmūd b. ʿUmar (d. 955/1548).[24] This leads him back to the point raised by al-Jirārī as to whether giving the benefit of the doubt by refraining from ownership of slaves in cases of doubt is a matter of scrupulousness (*al-waraʿ*) or a matter of law. For Aḥmad Bābā this should not be taken as a matter of scrupulousness, i.e. a matter of personal piety which leads one to avoid ownership out of fear of committing sin, but as a legal matter involving doubt over the reason for the person's being ownable, since the reason for enslavement is unbelief, and that is precisely what is in doubt.

Aḥmad Bābā then turns to the question of the Hamitic myth, which he proceeds to refute by reference to al-Suyūṭī's *Rafʿ shaʾn al-ḥubshān*—Ham's descendants settled in the southerly latitudes and became black, whereas Japheth's sons settled in the north and east and became red and blond—and to Ibn Khaldūn's earlier scornful refutation of the myth in favor of his theory of the effect of climate on skin color.[25] In response to the question about the "peculiarity [i.e. unique enslaveability]" of the "children of Ham," Aḥmad Bābā is quite clear: "This is not a peculiarity of theirs. Indeed, any unbeliever among the children of Ham,[26] or anyone else, may be possessed [as a slave] if he remains attached to his original unbelief. There is no difference between one race and another."

Having established the equality of black Africans with all other Muslims in this manner, Aḥmad Bābā then somewhat vitiates this by his interpretation of a *ḥadīth* cited by al-Jirārī: "Look after (*ittakhadhū*) the *sūdān*, for among them are three lords of the people of Paradise, Luqmān the Sage, al-Najāshī, and Bilāl the muezzin."[27] This apparently laudatory remark attributed to the Prophet is given a paternalistic interpretation: the Prophet asked his followers to look after, or be considerate to, black people so as to counteract the dislike they might have for such persons "on account of their objectionable characteristics, and their general lack of refinement." The Prophet, he says, gave such an order and encouraged people to follow it "because of the rapidity with which [the *sūdān*] are subdued and become obedient and go wherever they are driven, and the rapidity with which they embrace Islam, so that there might well be among them lords like those elect Muslims . . . ." Here Aḥmad Bābā first embraces certain stereotypes about black Africans—their "objectionable" characteristics and uncouthness, and their "servile" nature—but then attempts to redeem this by implicitly praising their rapid adoption of Islam, and by hinting that some of them might achieve the exalted status of the three "lords of Paradise" mentioned in the *ḥadīth*. But it can hardly be doubted that his thinking about black Africans (and we should not forget that, coming from Ṣanhāja Berber stock, he would have seen himself as belonging to the world, not of *sūdān*, but of *bīḍān*—"whites") was affected by notions of the inferiority and enslavability of black Africans, though his legal mind rejected the simple equivalence of blackness with slavery.

However in his reply to the next question of al-Jirārī about the *ḥadīth* "Your slaves are your brothers (*ikhwānukum khawalukum*)," he shows his humanity in relation to the matter of slavery, for he replies: "[T]here is in it an admonition to be kind and compassionate to him among them [sc. the *sūdān*] who is owned, as well as others, and to treat him kindly and compassionately, since the mere fact of being owned generally breaks one's heart because of the associated dominance and subordination, especially when people are far from home"; and he concludes: "All men are the sons of Adam. Hence [the Prophet] said: 'God caused you to own him, and had He wished, He would have caused him to own you,' or words to that effect, to alert you to His making his favor to you complete through Islam and His afflicting him [the slave], or his forebears with unbelief up to [the time when] he was captured."

Slavery, then, is a consequence of, and an affliction brought on by, being beyond the pale of Islam. It is the will of God that some folk should be Muslims and others not, and those who are Muslims should be aware that the situation might have been reversed. While this is a worthy admonition to Muslims to be considerate towards their slaves, it also legitimizes slavery inasmuch as it acknowledges Muslims' right to enslave non-Muslims, and, indeed, intimates that God in His wisdom created a situation in which some might be slaves of others, for had He so willed, He might have reversed the roles.

Black Slaves in State Service in Morocco

The creation of a large black slave army in Morocco is generally acknowledged to have been the work of Mūlāy Ismāʿīl (1672–1727), and it is not always realized that the origins of this force lie in the black slave corps assembled by Aḥmad al-Manṣūr (1578–1603), who obtained the bulk of them, it would seem, from within Morocco.[28] The arguments in favor of this development, and the justification for pressing blacks resident in Morocco into military service, are laid out by al-Manṣūr in an undated letter he addressed to the *ʿulamāʾ* of Egypt.[29] The argument begins by stating that Morocco is a land of fortresses and frontier posts (sing. *ribāṭ*), because it is close to the infidel enemy. Hence it needs to have a powerful army to defend it, and to defend Islam. In former times dynasty had succeeded dynasty and each one had always found a well-trained army, adequate war supplies, and a full treasury. Al-Manṣūr complains that he came to the throne at a time of weakness and found it emptied of armies and provisions and underpopulated, having suffered eighty years of strife and upheaval. He therefore began to see how he could build up a viable army. He continues:

> We found that free men in this age were unsuitable for military service on several counts, notably because they were

> overcome by inborn idleness, weakness, greed, and sensual desires. . . . We therefore left them to earn their livelihood, to pursue their interests and to pay taxes to the treasury. We turned to those slaves (*mamālīk*) and purchased them from their owners after searching for them and investigating them in accordance with the law and the observed *sunna*s. We found that many of these slaves were runaways who had deserted their owners and escaped from their control. Every one of them bore the runaway mark and was known by it, either through his father or his paternal or maternal grandparents . . . These runaways would attach themselves to other masters or to tribes, or become part of the entourage of shaykhs or big men with a following (*kabīr dh[ū] ʿaṣabiyya*), and defraud their owners who had [the right] of [their] clientship and were the original owners. Thus they became dispersed throughout the lands and regions, especially during times of dearth and turmoil when the shadow of the caliphate receded from these western regions, until famines and the passing of years consumed many of those slaves. This despite the fact that they are originally unbelieving blacks, imported from over there through purchase from those who neighbor them and raid them and campaign against them.

That al-Manṣūr faced a real problem to assemble an efficient and loyal army is certainly true. Earlier dynasties like the Marīnids, the Almohads and the Almoravids had been able to rely, to a large extent, upon a tribal base from which to recruit armies. Although the Saʿdians had done this during the conquest phase that brought them slowly to power over the first half of the sixteenth century, their tribal base was too limited to fulfill all the needs of the burgeoning Saʿdian state, especially given the hostile presence of the Ottomans on their eastern border, and the possibility (and in 1578 the reality) of invasion from the Iberian peninsula. Various solutions were found, including the recruitment of some Moroccan tribal peoples, and opening the doors to such non-Moroccans as Andalusians, "Turks" (i.e. Turkish-trained personnel of various origins), and European renegades (*ʿulūj*).

These were to be supplemented by black persons resident in Morocco, whose drafting into the army was justified on the specious grounds that all those blacks who were living at large in Moroccan society were in fact descendants of runaway slaves who had become clients of other men and deserted their original masters. They were, he argued, originally unbelievers who were captured in West Africa and sold in trade, and were bought and sold again in Morocco. Over time, during times of turmoil, they became dispersed, and some intermarried and produced offspring, not all of whom, al-Manṣūr is quick to point out, were the product of lawful marriage. Thus, in addition to being runaways, bastardy is also imputed to at least some of them.

Al-Manṣūr goes on to claim that he has conducted investigations into the origins of all these black slaves and has traced each one back to his original owner, and has determined that each one was originally lawfully purchased. But instead of returning the slaves to their lawful owners, al-Manṣūr asserts that since it is the duty of the ruler to obtain benefit for his people and the duty of subjects to accept the ruler's decisions in such matters, even when they do not understand the wisdom of such decisions,

> we selected those slaves to be made into soldiers and a channel (*zirb*) for Islam, because of qualities which they possess to the exclusion of others: they are a race (*jins*) who give little trouble, they are content with simple living conditions, accepting things as they find them without being troublesome or demanding. In addition, this race of slaves has strengthened this blessed affair of guarding the jihādist fortresses and encompassing the Islamic lands to which they were assigned and directed. They are tougher and more long-suffering over its movements and relocations. They were suited to that and best fitted to undertake it most perfectly.

Here again we encounter the stereotype which Aḥmad Bābā had evoked of black Africans being inherently servile, ready to obey, to put up with primitive conditions, and to be long-suffering about inconvenience. Indeed, in al-Manṣūr's argument, they are the ideal soldier because they are tough, take orders, and are willing to go anywhere. Rather surprisingly, later in the letter al-Manṣūr, in order further to justify his conscription of these black men, castigates them as being, before he recruited them, essentially criminals, engaged in highway robbery, kidnapping, embezzlement, theft, treachery, and heresy. This might seem to be somewhat at odds with the character required to make a good and loyal soldier. But taken together with his arguments about Moroccan blacks being runaways who have deserted their lawful masters and have (at least in some cases) multiplied through illicit sexual relationships, these further negative attributes serve to create the impression that they deserved no better fate than to be treated as slaves, and to be conscripted.

Lastly, al-Manṣūr sanctimoniously claims that recruiting them into his army is a way both of saving their souls, and of obtaining divine reward for himself:

> Additionally, we aimed to save them from the falling into the trap, in which son followed father, of being eternally cursed for taking as patrons persons other than their [original] patrons,[30] without their permission, as the *ḥadīth* indicates, that is: "Whoever becomes a client of people without the permission of his patrons, then upon him be the curse of God and His angels and all people . . . ." Also [we had] a desire to obtain a great reward from God Most High through civilizing them well and ordering them and training them and refining them. To this may be added the polishing they acquire in terms of good manners, fine qualities, and morals through their being attached to the *dīwān* and serving the household of the caliphate.

The slave is thus denied his personhood and individuality by finding his salvation not through his own deeds, but through his being, and remaining, attached to a free Muslim. His ability to be civilized on his own account is also denied him by al-Manṣūr's assertion that only through the slave's service in the royal army will he acquire good manners and morals.

Al-Manṣūr evidently found it necessary to present some sort of defense of his effective re-enslavement of blacks resident in Morocco, and for his acquiring possession of them against the putative claims of their original masters. He is at pains to stress that he has gone through the legal steps of tracing their ancestry, that all he is doing is to reassert their slave status, and that he has consulted with his *ʿulamāʾ*, who have approved his actions. But one is bound to suspect that there was considerable opposition to his actions and that some of the Moroccan *ʿulamāʾ* made their disagreements known. Why else would al-Manṣūr have turned to the *ʿulamāʾ* of Egypt for what he clearly expects will be a confirming opinion? The rest of the story is not, at this stage, known, but it is clear that his actions created an important precedent for Mūlāy Ismāʿīl almost a century later. Al-Manṣūr's letter also serves further to identify blackness with slavery in Morocco. For him there seems to have been no question of free blacks: all the blacks in Morocco were nothing more than runaway slaves.

The connection between the two black slave armies is made explicit in the account in the *kunnāsh* of Aḥmad al-Yaḥmadī, the vizier and head of chancery of Mūlāy Ismāʿīl, quoted in al-Nāṣirī's *Kitāb al-istiqṣāʾ*:

> When the sultan Mūlāy Ismāʿīl b. al-Sharīf conquered Marrakesh and entered it for the first time, he was enlisting his soldiers from among the free tribes. And then there came to him the secretary Abū Ḥafṣ ʿUmar b. Qāsim al-Marrākushī, called ʿAlīlīsh, whose family was one of leadership from ancient times. His father had been a secretary with al-Manṣūr al-Saʿdī and later with his sons. This Abū Ḥafṣ joined the service of Mūlāy Ismāʿīl and informed him about the register in which were the names of the slaves who were in the army of al-Manṣūr. The sultan asked him if any of them remained and he said, "Yes, and many of their descendants and they are scattered about in Marrakesh and its region (*ḥawz*) and among the tribes of the *dīr*.[31] If our lordship orders me to assemble them, I shall do so." So Mūlāy Ismāʿīl put him in charge of this and wrote on his behalf to the leaders of the tribes ordering them to support him and strengthen his arm as regards what he was about. ʿAlīlīsh set about searching for them in Marrakesh and making inquiries about their ancestry until he had assembled those of them

> who were there. Then he went out to the *dīr* and gathered those who were there. Then he went to the tribes of the *ḥawz* and rounded up whatever [blacks] there were among them until there no black was left among all those tribes, whether slave or *ḥarṭānī* [see below] or free. The drive became irreversible. In a single year he assembled 3,000, some married and others bachelors. Then he recorded them in a register and sent it to the sultan in Miknāsa. The sultan looked through it and was pleased with it, and he wrote to him ordering him to purchase slave women for the bachelors, and to pay the price of the slaves to their owners and to clothe them from the taxes (*aʿshār*) of Marrakesh, and bring them to him in Miknāsa.[32]

Once again the hapless blacks of Morocco were denied their chance to become integrated into the wider society and to live as free men and women. Sultan Mūlāy Ismāʿīl pursued the goal of a black slave army with relentless efficiency, draining the cities and tribes, and sending expeditions deep into the western Sahara. He not only rounded up men, but also purchased black women to whom he eventually married the men in order to produce a second generation of males who could be trained for military service and women who would serve in the royal household.[33] The assembled blacks are described throughout al-Yaḥmadī's account as "slaves" (*ʿabīd*), though it is clear from the above account that this was a sweep of all persons whose description responded to the notion of "black," since *ḥarāṭīn* (pl. of *ḥarṭānī*) and free blacks were also rounded up. Again, the notion that black Africans are inherently slaves seems to predominate.

It was, in fact, the question of the incorporation of *ḥarāṭīn* into the slave army that aroused the most vocal opposition. The whole question of the origins of the *ḥarāṭīn* is one shrouded in mystery; even the meaning of the term is in dispute.[34] One of the more plausible explanations is that in origin they represent the remains of aboriginal black populations of the Sahara.[35] They are to be found in most Saharan oases, among the Arab populations of Mauritania, in the villages of southern Morocco,[36] and in the seventeenth century, at any rate, in some Moroccan cities. Although they are of inferior social status and often function economically in client-type relationships, they are considered free; a folk etymology of their name—a deformation of *ḥurr thānī* (free in the second degree)—asserts as much, and in certain areas freed slaves may have been assimilated to them. According to Batran, many *ḥarāṭīn* had moved from Saharan oases into northern Moroccan cities in the wake of natural disasters and political upheavals.[37] Fez attracted a large number, who by 1690 were thoroughly urbanized, and some had married into Fāsī families. This did not deter Mūlāy Ismāʿīl from attempting to draft them into his slave army, the *ʿabīd al-Bukhārī.*

In a letter addressed to Sīdī Muḥammad b. ʿAbd al-Qādir al-Fāsī, Mūlāy Ismāʿīl made some of the same arguments that Aḥmad al-Manṣūr had made about the need for a loyal army to support the "caliphal" regime. Like him, too, he also asserted that the black slaves possessed the bravery, the resoluteness, the aptitude, and the endurance that are lacking in free men, and that once recruited they would dedicate their lives and energies to serving in the army.[38] He refused to make any distinction between *ḥarāṭīn* and slaves, present or past. For him, the *ḥarāṭīn* were simply slaves who had slipped the rope of servitude, which now ought to be reattached.

> No matter how long the Haratin, especially the brown-skin Haratin (*aḥmar al-jilda*) have been urbanized, many of them are, nonetheless, slaves. They have indeed severed all ties with their patrons and forgotten their (slave) origin. Some of them do not even know that they were originally slaves. Others are aware of this fact, but they will not acknowledge it, either because they do not wish to debase themselves after having become urbanized and have made a final break with their patrons and with those who know their origin, or because they hide behind baseless evidence in the Holy Law that proves that they are free born. We must, for this reason, investigate the background of the Haratin of Fas, so that every one of them will know his origin and his long forgotten patron.[39]

The *ʿulamāʾ* of Fez protested, but in vain, and one of their number,

Sīdī ʿAbd al-Salām b. Jāsūs paid for his principles with his life. His objection was founded on the premise that the basic presumption regarding human beings is their freedom, and that any claim to the contrary must be supported by incontrovertible evidence. Certainly, there was a need for a strong army to defend the Muslim state, but

> This does not mean the enslavement of free men, for joining the army is of one's own free will. [The forced recruitment of the *ḥarāṭīn* is] an unashamed enslavement of free men and reducing them to servitude with no legal justification. The Haratin of Fas are free like all other free born Muslims. Their free status is well known and is unquestionable. Therefore, any admission by them that they are slaves of named or unnamed persons, or any testimony given by others accusing them of being slaves, irrespective of why such testimony was presented, is indeed the result of pressure and coercion. This is witnessed and seen and there is no lack of evidence to support it. . . . Their admission to slavery, even if it were of their own volition and not forced on them, is invalid. According to the Holy Law they cannot be subjected to slavery nor bound by their own admission. Their freedom is a right Allah bestowed on them. Therefore they have no right to choose to be slaves.[40]

He argued that enslavement of free men was tantamount to a rejection of the *sharīʿa,* or at least to bringing it into contempt. It would also vitiate the act of manumitting slaves, which is a pious act and one beloved of the Prophet, since there could then be no guarantee that a manumitted slave would be allowed to live as a free Muslim. This, in turn, closed a door upon seeking closeness to God, which is the goal of such pious acts. This, he claimed, was a calamity which had uniquely befallen Morocco, and the generation of which he was a part.

The Strictures of the ʿUlamāʾ

The protest of ʿAbd al-Salām b. Jāsūs was in defiance of the Sultan, and hence he suffered the supreme penalty for his outspoken defense of the law. In the late nineteenth century, when abolition of slavery was the order of the day in neighboring Algeria and Tunisia, and in the Ottoman empire, a scholar such as Aḥmad b. Khālid al-Nāṣirī could speak his mind more freely, especially since he did so in the pages of a large work of history, and not in response to any state policy. But the attack he makes on his countrymen in general is a trenchant one, accusing them of hypocrisy, bad faith, and betraying the *sharīʿa.*

He launches this attack in his *Kitāb al-istiqṣāʾ* immediately after a long section on the Saʿdian conquest of the Middle Niger and an account of Aḥmad Bābā's deportation to Morocco.[41] He has, of course, read the latter's *Miʿrāj al-ṣuʿūd*, but argues that the work is of restricted application, since "this analysis which Shaykh Aḥmad Bābā made is only valid insofar as the people of the lands which border them [the people of the Middle Niger] are concerned and those who come across slaves brought from among them and others [beyond them]. As for the people of the Maghrib who are 'beyond what is beyond' [in relation to such peoples], and between whom and the land of the Sudan is a wide waterless desert and a wilderness inhabited only by the wind, who can ascertain the facts for them?" He asserts that the people of West Africa are by and large Muslims, and that this should be the basic assumption about them unless proved otherwise. To treat them, as Moroccans have habitually done, as enslavable unbelievers is a calamity:

> Thus will be apparent to you the heinousness of the affliction which has beset the lands of the Maghrib since ancient times in regard to the indiscriminate enslaving of the people of the Sūdān,[42] and the importation of droves of them every year to be sold in the market places in town and country where men trade in them as one would trade in beasts—nay worse than that. People have become so inured to that, generation after generation, that many common folk believe that the reason for being enslaved according to the Holy Law is merely that a man should be black in color and come from those regions. This, by God's life, is one of the foulest and gravest evils perpetrated upon God's religion, for the people of the Sūdān are

> Muslims having the same rights and responsibilities as ourselves. Even if you assume that some of them are pagans or belong to a religion other than Islam, nevertheless the majority of them today as in former times are Muslims, and judgment is made according to the majority. Again, even if you suppose that Muslims are not a majority and that Islam and unbelief claim equal members there, who among us can tell whether those brought here are Muslims or unbelievers. For the innate condition (*al-aṣl*) of humankind is freedom and lack of any cause for being enslaved. Whoever maintains the opposite is denying the basic condition.

One should not put any confidence in what the slave merchants say for they are "men of no morals, no manly qualities and no religion," and the evil nature of the age and the wickedness of its people are apparent. "Nor," he adds, "should any reliance be put upon the protestations of a slave man or woman, as the jurists have ruled, since motives and circumstances differ in this regard. A seller may do them so much ill that they would not admit to anything which would affect their sale. Or a slave may have the objective of getting out of the hands of his master by any possible means, thus finding it easy to admit to slave status so that the sale may be promptly effected. Other motives may also exist."

This last point echoes the dictum of earlier *ʿulamāʾ* cited by Ibn Jāsūs, namely that objective evidence is necessary to prove slave status, and people are not permitted to incriminate themselves in this regard. Finally, he points out that in the land of the *sūdān* there is much warfare, enslavement, and kidnapping, and by implication, many Muslims end up in slavery.[43] "How then can a man who has scruples about his religion permit himself to buy something of this nature? How too can he allow himself to take their women as concubines, considering that this involves entering upon a sexual liaison of doubtful legality?" This last point brings us back again to ʿAbd al-Raḥmān al-Saʿdī's ancestor, who, rather than risk the sin of fornication with a captured Fulani (and hence almost certainly Muslim) woman, married her in preference to taking her as a concubine.

Old attitudes die hard. Sometime during the closing years of the nineteenth century an otherwise obscure scholar, most probably from

Timbuktu, Muḥammad al-Sanūsī b. Ibrāhīm al-Jārimī, wrote a treatise attacking Moroccans who considered black Africans to be slaves *sui generis*. The treatise, entitled *Tanbīh ahl al-ṭughyān ʿalā ḥurriyyat al-sūdān* ["Alerting Tyrannical Folk to the Free Status of the *sūdān*"], seems to have been written between 1312/1894–95 and 1316/1898. The first date is the date of publication, very shortly after its completion, of al-Nāṣirī's *Kitāb al-istiqsāʾ*, from which al-Jārimī quotes. The latter date is the year in which the only known copy of this work was made.[44] After an introduction al-Jārimī begins his treatise as follows:

> When I traveled to the land of the Farther Maghrib [Morocco] . . . I found some of the uncouth Maghribīs claiming that all blacks without exception were slaves who did not deserve to be free, for how should they deserve that, being black of skin? On this matter they relate fantasies that have no foundation to them in law or the natural order (*al-ṭabʿ*). As for the law, nothing came down from the lawgiver that would explain why among all peoples (*umam*) they should be enslaved rather than others. With regard to nature, [such an argument is unacceptable] because the natural order rejects blacks being slaves without a compelling legal reason.[45]

After a detailed rebuttal of the notion of the superiority of "red over black" (or vice-versa) supported especially by *ḥadīth* texts, he takes up the argument made by some Moroccans that blacks are unfit to govern themselves independently, since they lack order and unity. He observes that their ability to govern themselves is not the point at issue—what they do as free persons is their own affair. In any case, they are not apparently dependent on anyone in managing their affairs. If one were to argue that they have been conquered by the Christians, then at the time of writing this was also true of the people of Algeria, Tunisia, and Syria, and (though he does not make the point explicitly) no one argues that they are incapable of governing themselves and deserve to be enslaved.

Al-Jārimī's final reprimand, though perhaps at the extreme of general discourse about race and slavery, does drive home the point that he, and others before him, had made about the widespread Moroccan belief in the innate servility of black Africans. A man had argued that marrying more than four black women concomitantly was not a breach of the *sharīʿa*, even though he had married them in regular fashion, seeking their hands through their fathers (as guardians) and paying the bride-price (*ṣadāq*). His argument was simple: they were black and hence, *ipso facto*, unfree. Indeed, the word "freedom" and the word "black" were mutually exclusive; to apply it to them would be to use a concept that had no reality behind it (*ism bi-la musammā*).

Al-Jārimī, however, should have the last word:

> [T]his contradicts the view of the mass (*jumhūr*) of the scholars to the effect that the innate condition of people is freedom (*al-aṣl fī 'l-nās huwa 'l-ḥurriyya*); indeed some have stated that there is consensus (*ijmāʿ*) [over this]. If the man claims [lawfulness of five black wives] willfully and by way of declaring the forbidden to be licit, then this is deviance (*ilḥād*) and unbelief. The one who denies something over which there is consensus and which is of necessity known, is certainly an unbeliever.[46]

Notes

1. Bernard Lewis, *Race and Slavery in the Middle East* (New York, 1990), 99–102. See also William J. Sersen, "Stereotypes and attitudes towards slaves in Arabic proverbs: a preliminary view," in *Slaves and Slavery in Muslim Africa*, ed. John Ralph Willis (London, 1985), 1:92–105; Leon Carl Brown, "Color in northern Africa," *Daedalus* 96 (Spring 1967), 464–82; L. Blin, "Les noirs dans l'Algérie contemporaine," *Politique Africaine* 30 (juin 1988), 22–31; Albertine Jwaideh and J. W. Cox, "The black slaves of Turkish Arabia during the 19th century," *Slavery and Abolition* 9:3 (1988), 45–59, where (speaking of Iraq) they remark: "The distinction between *ḥurr* and *ʿabd* was binding and unalterable. It was a case of once an *ʿabd* always an *ʿabd*, whether manumitted or not. And while not all *ʿabīd* were black, the terms for negro and slave were used interchangeably."
2. See, for example, the reflections of a black Turkish woman, Ayse Birkan, in *Daughters of Africa*, ed. Margaret Busby (London, 1992), 884. Although she asserts that it is religion and not color that divides people in the Muslim world, she admits "there is some racism in Turkey."

3. In a *fatwā* included in al-Wansharīsī's *Mi'yār* (fifteenth century North Africa), slavery is described as "a humiliation and a servitude caused by previous or current unbelief and having as its purpose to discourage unbelief." See Bernard Lewis, op. cit., 148.

4. A recommended formula in a manumission document is *wa-alḥaqahu bi-aḥrār al-muslimīn, lahu mā lahum wa-'alayhi mā 'alayhim*—"He [the owner] has made him one with the free Muslims, partaking both of their privileges and their responsibilities"; see John Hunwick, "Falkeiana IV: the *Kitāb al-tarsīl*, an anonymous manual of epistolatory and notary style," *Sudanic Africa* 5 (1994), 181.

5. Aḥmad b. Khālid al-Nāṣirī al-Salāwi, *K. al-istiqṣā' li-akhbār duwal al-maghrib al-aqṣā* (Casablanca, 1955–56), 5:131.

6. On these rules, see Rudolph Peters, *Jihād in Classical and Modern Islam* (Princeton, 1996). In the West African context, see 'Uthmān b. Fūdī, *Bayān wujūb al-hijra 'alā 'l-'ibād*, ed. and trans. F.H. Elmasri (Khartoum-Oxford, 1978). The ruler who fought resistant unbelievers had several options in regard to male captives: to kill them, to enslave them, to ransom them, or to pardon them. Women and children could not be killed.

7. See John O. Hunwick, "Askia al-Ḥājj Muḥammad and his successors: the account of al-Imām al-Takrūrī," *Sudanic Africa* 1 (1990), 85–90. The name of the caliph is not mentioned, but al-Mustamsik was caliph (for the first time) 903/1497–914/1508. See C.E. Bosworth, *The Islamic Dynasties* (Edinburgh, 1967), 8.

8. See al-Nāṣirī, *K. al-istiqṣā'*, 5:104–11. In the *bay'a* document prepared for Mai Idrīs's signature, Sultan Aḥmad al-Manṣūr's secretary makes much of his caliphal claims, referring to his being honored with *al-khilāfa al-nabawiyya wa 'l-imāma al-Ḥasaniyya al-'Alawiyya*.

9. On Makhlūf al-Balbālī, see *Arabic Literature of Africa*, Vol. II, *The Writings of Central Sudanic Africa*, compiled by John O. Hunwick (Leiden, 1995), 25.

10. He says that similar judgments had been given by jurists of Andalusia and Fez. Quotations from al-Balbālī's *fatwā* are taken from a draft translation by Fatima Harrak and John Hunwick being prepared for eventual publication together with the *Mi'rāj al-ṣu'ūd* of Aḥmad Bābā and other documents relating to slavery in North and West Africa.

11. 'Abd al-Raḥmān b. 'Imrān al-Sa'dī, *Ta'rīkh al-sūdān*, ed. and trans. O. Houdas (Paris, 1898–1900), 67. In order to marry her he would have had first to free her.

12. 'Afnū is a Kanuri term for the Hausa who border Bornu in the west. See

John Lavers, "A note on the terms 'Hausa' and "ʿAfnu."" *Kano Studies* (n.s.), 2:1 (1980), 113–20.

13. Arab writers of the medieval period generally write the name "Gao" as "Kawkaw," to be pronounced "Gawgaw," though a late Ibāḍī source spells it "Jawjaw." See John O. Hunwick, *Sharīʿa in Songhay* (Oxford, 1985), 3. The spelling "Jūghū" could be pronounced "Gawghaw."

14. I.e., if there is doubt about a factor that may change an existing condition, then the condition should not be changed.

15. In this case, if there is a known condition and there is doubt whether that condition has been changed, then no change should be accepted. Since the basic condition of human beings is liberty, then this condition is presumed to exist in the absence of proof to the contrary.

16. *Azhār al-ʿurūsh fī akhbār al-ḥubūsh* is al-Suyūṭī's own abridgement and reworking of his *Rafʿ sha'n al-ḥubshān*, for which see below, n. 18.

17. While the plural form *sūdān* literally only means "black," it also takes on a quasi-ethnic sense, inasmuch as the term *al-sūdān* refers to black Africans in general, and hence Africa to the immediate south of the Sahara was know as *bilād al-sūdān*—"lands of the *sūdān*."

18. See Ibn Khaldūn, *al-Muqaddima*, trans. F. Rosenthal, 2nd ed. (Princeton, 1967), 1:172–73. See also Saud H. al-Khathlan, "A critical edition of *Rafʿ sha'n al-ḥubshān* by Jalāl al-Dīn al-Suyūṭī" (Ph.D. diss., St Andrews University, 1983), Arabic text, p. 6, where al-Suyūṭī quotes a *ḥadīth* on the authority of Abū Hurayra in which the Prophet defines the descendants of Shem as the Arabs, the Persians, and the Byzantines, the descendants of Japheth as the Turks, the Slavs, and "Gog and Magog," and the descendants of Ham as the Copts, the Berbers and the *sūdān*. See also Abū 'l-Fidā' Ismāʿīl b. Kathīr, *Qiṣaṣ al-anbiyā'* (Beirut, 1408/1987), 86–87.

19. Quotations from Aḥmad Bābā are taken from the draft translation by Fatima Harrak and John Hunwick (see n. 10 above). The only text and translation in print, which is unsatisfactory in many ways, is Bernard Barbour and Michelle Jacobs, "The *Miʿrāj*: a legal treatise on slavery by Ahmad Baba," in J.R. Willis, ed., *Slaves and Slavery in Muslim Africa* (London, 1985), i, 125–59.

20. He confesses he does not know anything about ʿAfnū, and has never heard of it.

21. See Ibn Khaldūn, *Kitāb al-ʿibar wa-dīwān al-mubtada' wa 'l-khabar* (Būlāq, 1284/1867), 6:199–200, trans. in J.F.P. Hopkins and N. Levtzion, *Corpus of Early Arabic Sources for West African History* (Cambridge, 1981), 332–33. Ibn Khaldūn's account of the Berber (Ṣanhāja/Almoravid) conquest of

Ghana seems to fly in the face of Aḥmad Bābā's arguments, but he glosses over this.

22. I.e. Zaria in northern Nigeria. At the end of his treatise, in response to al-Jirārī's pressing for more detailed information, he provides a further insight into the religious ethnography of West Africa when he lists as persistent unbelievers the following groups: Mossi, Gurma, Busa, Borgu, Dagomba, Kotokoli, Yoruba, hill Dogon (text: Tunbughu=Tombo), Bobo, Karmū (?), and the Kumbē (Dogon of the plains), "except for a few of the people of Hombori and Daʿanka (Douentza?), though their Islam is shallow, so there is no harm in possessing them without posing questions." In a second reply to al-Jirārī, however, he states that the last two groups are "free Muslims" and should not be held as slaves. A much more detailed list of Muslim and non-Muslim groups appears in one manuscript as a postscript to Aḥmad Bābā's second reply to al-Jirārī, but the authorship and date of this are in doubt.

23. An Andalusian Mālikī, *qāḍī* of Tangiers, Miknās, and Granada at various times, d. 486/1093–94. See Ibn Farḥūn, *al-Dībāj al-mudhahhab fi maʿrifat aʿyān ʿulamāʾ al-madh'hab* (Cairo, 1351/1932–33), 181–82.

24. See Aḥmad Bābā, *Nayl al-ibtihāj bi-taṭrīz al-dībāj*, on marg. of Ibn Farḥūn, *al-Dībaj al-mudhahhab*, 343–44. We do not have any written record of *qāḍī* Maḥmūd's view, but Aḥmad Bābā, who reports it, was his great-nephew, and would certainly have been aware of such a judgment.

25. On the Hamitic myth, see Edith Sanders, "The Hamitic hypothesis: its origin and functions in time perspective," *J. African History* 10 (1969), 521–32. For a discussion of this article and a more critical reading of the post-Biblical sources, see Ephraim Isaac, "Genesis, Judaism, and the 'Sons of Ham,'" in *Slaves and Slavery in Muslim Africa*, ed. John Ralph Willis, 1:75–91; Bernard Lewis, op. cit., 123–25. See also William McKee Evans, "From the land of Canaan to the land of Guinea: the strange odyssey of the 'sons of Ham,'" *American Historical Review* 85 (1980), 15–43. On the *Rafʿ shaʾn al-ḥubshān* of al-Suyūṭī, see Akbar Muhammad, "The image of Africans in Arabic literature: some unpublished manuscripts," in *Slaves and Slavery in Muslim Africa*, 1:47–74, and al-Khathalan, op. cit.; on Ibn Khaldūn's theories about skin color, see his *Muqaddima*, trans. F. Rosenthal, 1:167–73, discussed in John O. Hunwick, *West Africa and the Arab World: Historical and Contemporary Perspectives* (Accra, 1991), 6–9.

26. It is not only the *sūdān* who are generally considered to be the "children of Ham." Arab authors generally include the Copts and the Berbers; see, for example, Ibn Qutayba, *Kitāb al-maʿārif*, ed. F. Wüstenfeld (Göttingen, 1850), 13–14; Shams al-Dīn al-Dimashqī, *Nukhbat al-dahr fī ʿajāʾib al-barr*

wa'l-baḥr, ed. M.A.F. Mehren (Leipzig, 1923), 266. Translations of these passages may be found in Hopkins and Levtzion, *Corpus*, 15 and 212 respectively. Ibn Qutayba also makes the people of "Hind and Sind" descendants of Ham.

27. Luqmān is generally considered by Muslim tradition to have been an Ethiopian or Nubian slave, but proverbially wise, and according to some, a prophet. See B. Heller - [N. Stillman], art. "Luḳmān," *Encyclopaedia of Islam*, 2nd edn., Leiden, 1960– [in progress], hereafter *EI* (2), 5:812; al-Ṭabarī, *Jāmiʿ al-bayān ʿan taʾwīl al-Qurʾān* (Cairo, 1383/1954), 21:67–68. The term Najāshī in Arabic (derived from Geʿez: negâsî), is strictly a title meaning king, but has come in Muslim tradition to be used as the name of the Ethiopian ruler who received the Muslim emigrants from Mecca. He is also (as in al-Suyūṭī's *Rafʿ shaʾn al-ḥubshān*) given the personal name of Aṣḥama, or some variant of it. See E. van Donzel, art. "al-Nadjāshī," *EI* (2), 8:862. Bilāl b. Rabāḥ was a freedman of Abū Bakr, and an early convert to Islam, who attached himself to the Prophet and became the first muezzin in Islam. He is generally accepted to have been of "Ethiopian" descent.; see *EI* (2), 1:1215.

28. Some were, perhaps, slaves sent back by the Saʿdian expedition that defeated Songhay in 1591. See M. Delafosse, "Les débuts des troupes noires au Maroc," *Hespéris* 3 (1923), 1–12, who, however, says of al-Manṣūr, "il n'apparait pas qu'il ait songé à constituer un corps spécialement formé de soldats noirs."

29. See the *kunnāsha* of Sultan Mūlāy ʿAbd al-Ḥafīẓ, entitled *Dāʾ al-ʿaṭb al-qadīm*, ms. 400-11z, Royal Library (al-Khizāna al-Ḥasāniyya), Rabat.

30. Legally, their patrons are the persons who manumitted them, in accordance with the well-known dictum *al-walāʾ li-man aʿtaq*.

31. G. Deverdun describes al-Ḥawz as "the region of Marrakesh, the Haouz, a wide embanked plain drained by the *wādī* Tansift with its tributaries, and by the *wādī* Tassawt," while *al-dīr* is the foothill region of the Atlas mountains. See *EI* (2), 3:300–301, art. "Ḥawz."

32. Al-Nāṣirī, *Kitāb al-istiqṣāʾ*, 7:56–57. Al-Manṣūr died in 1603, and Mūlāy Ismāʿīl came to the throne in 1672, so there can hardly have been any black soldier who served in al-Manṣūr's army alive in Ismāʿīl's time. At best those rounded up would have been sons of such soldiers, and more likely grandsons.

33. The black army he eventually assembled has been generally known as the *ʿabīd al-Bukhārī*, because the soldiers swore an oath of loyalty on a copy of the *ḥadīth* collection of al-Bukhārī, *al-Jāmiʿ al-Ṣaḥīḥ*. For the modern liter-

ature on them, see Magaly Morsy, "Maulay Ismail et l'armée de métier," *Revue de l'histoire moderne et contemporaine* 14 (1967), 97–122; Allan R. Meyers, "The ʿAbīd al-Bukhārī: slave soldiers and statecraft in Morocco" (Ph.D. diss., Cornell University, 1974); idem, "Class, ethnicity and slavery: the origins of the Moroccan ʿabīd," *Int. J. African Hist. Stud.* 10 (1977), 427–42; idem, "Slave soldiers and state politics in early ʿAlawī Morocco, 1668–1727," *Int. J. African Hist. Stud.* 16 (1983), 39–48. On the black palace slaves of the nineteenth century, see Mohammed Ennaji, *Soldats, domestiques et concubines: l'esclavage au Maroc au XIXe siècle* (Casablanca, 1994). Their free descendants still serve.

34. See G. Colin, art. "Ḥarṭānī," in *EI* (2), 3:230; D. Jacques-Meunié, "Hiérarchie sociale au Maroc présaharien," *Hespéris* 65 (1958), 252, relates the word *ḥarṭānī* to the Berber *aḥarḍane* meaning "black."

35. G. Camps, "Recherches sur les origines des cultivateurs noirs du Sahara," *Revue de l'occident musulman et de la Méditerranée* 7 (1970), 35–45.

36. See Jacques-Meunié, op. cit.

37. A.A. Batran, "The ʿUlamāʾ of Fez, M. Isma'il and the issue of the Haratin of Fas," in *Slaves and Slavery in Muslim Africa*, 2:1–15.

38. Batran, op. cit., 2.

39. Batran, op. cit., 5.

40. The *fatwā* is translated in Batran, op. cit., 9–13. The passage above is from his translation.

41. Al-Nāṣirī, *K. al-istiqṣāʾ*, 5:131–34. The quotations in the following paragraphs are taken from the translation of this entire passage appearing in J.O. Hunwick, "Black Africans in the Islamic world," *Tarikh* 5:4 (1978), 38–40. See also Lewis, *Race and Slavery*, 57–58.

42. "Sūdān" is shorthand for *bilād al-sūdān*—the land of the blacks.

43. There is clear evidence of West African Muslims having been enslaved and transported across the Atlantic to the United States and Brazil; see, for example, *Africa Remembered: Narratives by West Africans from the Era of the Slave Trade*, ed. Philip D. Curtin (Madison, 1966); Allan D. Austin, *African Muslims in Antebellum America* (New York, 1984); Joao José Reis, *Slave Rebellion in Brazil: the Muslim Uprising of 1835 in Bahia*, trans. Arthur Brakel (Baltimore, 1993).

44. This copy is preserved in the Centre de Documentation et de Recherches Historiques Ahmed Baba, Timbuktu [Mali], ms. no. 1575.

45. *Tanbīh ahl al-ṭughyān*, f. 2r.

46. *Tanbīh*, ff. 8v–9r.

Translation of Louis Frank's *Mémoire sur le commerce des nègres au Kaire, et sur les maladies auxquelles ils sont sujets en y arrivant* (1802)[1]

(Memoir on the Traffic in Negroes in Cairo
and on the Illnesses to which they are Subject upon arrival there)

MICHEL LE GALL

The translated text that follows was first published in Paris in 1802. It is the work of Dr. Louis Frank (1761–1825), a French physician of German origin who trained at Göttingen and later at the University of Pavia in Italy. In 1796 Frank emigrated from Milan, where he worked at the hospital, to Florence following the French invasion of northern Italy. For reasons that are not entirely clear, he left for Egypt in the fall of 1797 and traveled through the country almost as far south as Aswan. With the French invasion of 1798 Frank was—as were all other Europeans in Egypt—detained by the Mamluk authorities. After the victory of French forces, he was released and through contacts at the "Mission d'Egypte"—the French scientific expedition based in Cairo—he was appointed by commander Bonaparte as physician of the army of the Orient at the military hospital in Alexandria.

Following the French withdrawal from Egypt in 1801, Dr. Frank returned to Paris. Unsuccessful in winning Bonaparte's favor a second time, he set out for Tunis in 1802. He remained there for a year, found his way back to France, and then set out again for Italy. From there he traveled to Albania to present his credentials to Ali Arslan Pasha of Janina whom he served until 1806 as personal physician and public health officer. In 1810, he once again returned to Paris to work the patronage networks. On this occasion, he won the post of physician-in-chief of the hospital on the Ionian island of Corfu. The fall of Napoleon in 1812 precipitated Frank's sudden repatriation. With the help of an uncle, Frank traveled to Vienna in 1816 where he assumed the responsibility of court physician to Marie-Louise, former empress of France. There, he married an Austrian woman and established a school of anatomy and an asylum for the insane. He died on May 19, 1825.

The value of Frank's brief treatise on the slave trade in Cairo lies in two aspects. The first is the purely descriptive account that he offers about the slave trade, the attitudes and prejudices of slave owners and dealers, and his review of the diseases and problems encountered by slaves as they moved from the limited biological environment of the Sudan to the more disease-prone Mediterranean world. On a second level, Dr. Frank's mémoire provides a glimpse into the attitudes of an early nineteenth-century European observer of slavery in the Islamic world. Although repulsed by the practice of slavery, Frank unconsciously concedes that the fate of slaves in Cairo is far better than that of the plantation slaves in the New World, both French and American. Indeed, one can almost detect in Frank's tone a certain "Republican" appreciation of the fact that slavery in Islamic world seemed to respect the person—if not the rights—of the slave in a fashion unknown in the West.

Everything related to the trade in Negroes, in which various European nations have been engaged since the beginning of the sixteenth century on the Guinea Coast, is generally known; but it is astonishing that for all the famous travelers who have visited Egypt none has spoken in their travel accounts of the trade in Negroes conducted in Cairo which, from all appearances, is very old. As this topic seemed interesting to me, and to have some merit for those interested in the history of peoples, I made a special effort to gather together all that pertains to the trade in Negroes in the largest known city in Africa, in which I resided for almost five years.

Travelers have advanced a number of statements, often appalling, on the causes which force Negroes, in their native country, to fall into slavery. I have, for my part, tried to carry out exact researches on this topic. Four different causes appear to be the most frequent.

1. War which, according to all the information that I obtained from the Negroes themselves, arises from the frequent quarrels among their kings or their sultans, that invariably are ended by the force of arms. All then belongs to the victor; the subjects of the vanquished become his captives and they are either kept in his service or are sold or exchanged for commodities such as linen, towels, clothing, cows, camels, horses, etc.

When the Negroes go to war all the family members follow their respective chiefs; even their wives, whether from devotion or from duty, are included. Consequently, the followers of an army are usually far greater in number than the fighting men.

Mr. Browne, in his account of the kingdom of Darfur,[2] relates that when the sultan of Teraub set out to attack Kordofan, he had 500 women in his retinue and he had left an equal number at home. Some had the job of grinding grain, of drawing water, or of preparing the food. Apart from the king's concubines, all of them traveled on foot and carried part of the baggage on their heads.

After the famous battle of the Pyramids, the Negroes and Negresses whom the Mamluks had abandoned with their families in their defeat, admired and praised those Frenchmen who did not exercise the rights of victor over them and sometimes allowed Negresses to dine with them and even to share their beds. Their admiration was even greater since the French had been represented to them as the most inhuman and savage people.

2. The kidnapping of some individuals, which is done even from one hut to another, brings a somewhat smaller number of these unhappy wretches into a state of slavery.

Mischief, audacity, and the habit of stealing from one's fellows sometimes goes so far among them that children have been reported kidnapped while lying at the very side of their mother. A Negro who had been in one of these huts, normally made of cane, took note of the place where the mother usually slept with her daughter aged about three. A few days later this same Negro came during the night, skillfully parted the canes, and took the little Negro girl in her sleep without the unfortunate mother becoming aware of it.

3. Another group of Negro slaves are taken among wandering hordes who have no religion and no form of government. Others, under the rule of some sultan, better educated in the art of destroying their fellow men, armed with muskets and other weapons follow the trails of these hordes which are fairly common and try to blockade them and in particular to deprive them of water. This blockade, or to be more precise, this manhunt, can be fairly long. The besieged, as soon as they realize that they are surrounded, defend themselves with stones; the besiegers on the other hand do no more than fire an occasional musket shot to frighten them. These unfortunate souls, overcome by hunger and thirst, are finally obliged to surrender to their eager oppressors after liberal assurances that nothing will befall them. Each of the besiegers seizes a number of these wretches, binds them with cords and chains, and takes them home, where they are exchanged for other commodities.

4. Mr. Browne mentions a fourth cause of slavery. Whenever a man allows himself even the slightest appearance of trespass on the property of another, his punishment is to have his children or the youngest members of his family reduced to slavery. Worse, if a man sees the footprint of another in his fields, he calls witnesses, lodges a complaint before a magistrate, and once the case is proven, it inevitably costs the offender his son, his nephew, or his niece, whom he is obliged to surrender to the offended party. These incidents which constantly recur cannot fail to produce a great number of slaves. The same punishment is meted out to anyone who, entrusted with making purchases in a distant market, does not exactly carry out the task entrusted to him.

The idea, widespread in Europe, that fathers and mothers or relatives sell their children in the market to the highest bidder is absolutely false. They attach as much value to their children as do the most civilized nations. "If you white men are capable of believing such absurd stories," said a Negro to me one day, "then you should not be astonished if, among ignorant people like us, so many absurd beliefs prevail about the character, manners, and customs of your nation. All animals are grieved when their young ones are taken from them; why would you rank us below all beasts?"

When a father dies and leaves a large family without means and without relatives capable of supporting them, the sultan often takes the children on the pretext of making servants of them and compensates the mother or other persons who would have supported them. Thus he acquires individuals whom he eventually sells to merchants dealing with Egypt. I think that this practice may have given rise to the story that Negroes sell their children in the market like domestic animals.

The *Ghellabi*s[3] or slave traders can only go to Egypt in a more or less sizable caravan. The sultan appoints one or two caravan chiefs whom they call *el-Habirri*.[4] They are entrusted not only with maintaining order but further with selling the slaves as well as other products of their country on the sultan's account; and with the proceeds of their sales they buy articles of clothing, weapons etc. in Cairo. The provision of food for the Negroes consists of a type of Turkish wheat or maize which they call *Dourra*.[5] Since the camels of the caravan are burdened with water or with gum-arabic, elephant tusks, tamarind, pots, etc., all the Negroes with the exception of children up to the age of ten or twelve are obliged to follow on foot. If at the moment when the caravan departs, the *Ghellabi*s do not take great precautions, many of their Negroes escape. The certainty of never again seeing their native land and the fear of being mistreated by the whites induce them to flee, though the merchants use all their eloquence to persuade them that they will be much better off with foreigners than at home. For the rest, the *Ghellabi*s are usually people of a completely inhuman disposition who have more regard for their camels than for their Negroes. If on the way, these do not follow, they make them walk faster by means of a whip or *cortbatche*.[6] Those who wish to cross in greater comfort the desert separating Egypt from the Sudan buy donkeys, which are the best mount, and a parasol made out of oil cloth. The caravan always sets out at daybreak and stops only towards evening. Then some light fires while others grind a portion of *dourra* on a concave stone, which is part of their cooking utensils, and then cook it into a gruel with a very small quantity of salted beef jerky. Lunch likewise consists of a mash of *dourra* but without meat. They are remarkably sparing with water; often the wretched Negroes are only allowed to drink once a day, as a result of which more of them die of thirst than of exhaustion. This way of saving water, in itself so cruel, is dictated by two powerful circumstances. The first is that during a crossing of 36 to 40 days they find water only three or four times, that is to say every ten to twelve days; the second is that often a large number of water-bearers die. Despite all these obstacles, it has been established that the number of Negroes that die on this exhausting journey is infinitely smaller than that sustained in the traffic in Negroes on the Guinea Coast.

Before the arrival of the French, the caravans of Sennar and Darfur stopped at Abu Tig, a little town in Upper Egypt, where it was the practice of the *Ghellabis*, because of their insatiable greed, to have eunuchs made. Curious to know all about this cruel operation, I inquired of the governor of this town. He assured me that they made from one to two hundred eunuchs a year; that the death rate among them was not very significant, and that healing took place relatively quickly. A eunuch normally is sold for double the price of another Negro, and it is this increase in price which prompts the owners, or more appropriately, usurpers to have some of these unfortunate people mutilated. As concerns the procedure of the operation itself, I was unable to obtain very precise or definite information. Nevertheless, the essential is that with one hand the person performing the procedure grasps the scrotum and penis which he extends slightly, then, with a razor in the other hand, he removes everything in a single stroke. This operation, although in itself very simple, requires a certain dexterity and experience: for if the operator stretches the parts too much or cuts them too close, the patient may easily die. If, on the other hand, he does not stretch them enough, a kind of stump will result which leaves the eunuch deformed and which will not fail to alarm a prospective buyer. I do not know the means by which the flow of blood is stopped after the cutting of the parts. Some told me that they applied mule's dung; others that the patient was buried up to the waist in a ditch which was then filled with sand. If in the course of so bizarre a treatment the urethra remains free, the patient has some hope of healing. If, on the other hand, it is blocked, there follows a suppression of the flow of urine which soon leads to death.

In whatever manner this cruel operation is carried out, it is astonishing that the death rate is so low. This evidently results from the strong constitution of the Negroes and the age at which they are subjected to this operation; for they are ordinarily chosen among children of eight to ten and never above. Pietro della Valle[7] reports, however, that in Persia those who are subjected to this operation as a punishment for rape or other crimes of this kind recover very well, even if advanced in age, and that the only treatment is some ashes on the wound.

In the Barbary states, they simply apply liquefied tar to the wound. I have often chatted with eunuchs in Cairo; but none of them was willing to give me accurate information on the operation they had undergone; they constantly avoided the question in an effort to persuade me that they had lost all recollection of it.

The arrival of the French army in Egypt spontaneously stopped the barbaric practice of mutilating Negroes in such an inhuman fashion. By virtue of an order of General Bonaparte, the commanders of the troop corps stationed in Upper Egypt bought, when a caravan stopped there, the Negroes who might be apt for military service. And experience has shown that they are just as capable of becoming good soldiers as are Europeans.

In Synt the *Ghellabis* were obliged to pay to the Mamluks a due of about 24 to 30 francs for each Negro and each camel; they were then given a certificate without which they could not enter Cairo with their merchandise.

There are only three caravans which bring Negroes to Cairo: the first is that from Sennar; the second that from Darfur; and the third, the one called Moghrabi, or the western caravan which comes from Murzuq, capital of Fezzan and sometimes from Bornu and other times from Havnia.[8] The first two caravans normally come once a year; the one from Fezzan sometimes comes only every two years.

When a caravan arrives in Cairo, it takes its Negroes as well as all its other merchandise to a *wikala* or special caravansary, generally known under the name of Negro market, which is remarkable only for its dilapidated state and its great filth. The two sexes are separated in nasty little rooms that very much resemble our prisons. Others are placed in groups in the courtyard of the *wikala,* often on the merchandise of their masters. The first time a European sees this market with the Negroes, most of whom are naked, boys and girls of every age, even mothers with infants stuck at their breasts, he can hardly resist the painful feelings that such a spectacle causes him. But if one goes there often, if one observes the merriment that reigns among these captives, their carefreeness, and if one thinks that they are shortly to enter into a kinder world and that they are at the end of their suffering, one gradually gets used to looking at them with much less pain.

All that is usually said in Cairo about the number of Negroes sold there every year is absolutely exaggerated. I took the trouble to inform myself about this subject with the proprietor of the *wikala* in addition to the Coptic scribe who has been registering for thirty years all the Negroes that are sold there. But neither was able to give me exact information, either because they are not interested or because, instead of preserving the registers, they burn them every year. Nevertheless, in comparing all that trustworthy people have told me about this subject, it appears that in the past they used to sell at most three or four thousand of both sexes.[9] But since, for some time, the Mamluks have continually imposed even greater taxes, the traders have become so disgusted with Egypt that at the time of my arrival in Cairo (in the year 6),[10] they were hardly bringing more than twelve hundred Negroes a year. In the past, caravans brought from 1,000 to 1,500 Negroes, but more recently the number was no more than about 600. In the course of the three and a half years that the French were masters of Egypt, only four not very large caravans arrived. But there is every reason to believe that if we had kept this country, the *Ghellabis* would have come more frequently with large caravans.

It is the custom of the inhabitants of Cairo to judge that a Negro is of good character when they have fine eyes and the whites of their eyes are very white and when they have red gums and tongues without brown or blackish discoloration, the palms of the hands and the soles of the feet pink, and handsome nails. They maintain that the Negroes whose white of the eye is brown or reddish, and whose tongue and gums have black stains, are of bad disposition and are completely incorrigible. I do not have sufficient experience to confirm or refute this assertion, but I can certainly vouch that I have encountered Negroes and Negresses with the all the physical defects mentioned above who in no way were of poor disposition; and I have seen others with all the requisite physical qualities who had an absolutely perverse character.

Many of the inhabitants of Cairo, and even Negroes, told me that one sometimes encountered among the Negroes offered for sale some who are cannibals and that they can be recognized by a little tail or a prolongation of the coccyx bone. They further told me that the *Ghellabis* removed it when they observed it and it was therefore essential to examine carefully to see if there was any scar in the place indicated. I took a great deal of trouble to confirm this fact, but I was only able to obtain unsatisfactory answers. Among a large number of persons of standing whom I asked if they had seen this kind of Negro *with their own eyes*, there was none who could reply affirmatively to my question.

The Negroes who come with the Sennar caravan are originally from Nubia; they are not completely black and often have regular features. For these reasons, the girls from these regions sometimes pass for Abyssinians because they are more sought after. But the fact is that the Sennar caravan brings only a very small number of slaves captured, at the very most, near the frontiers of Abyssinia. Those who are in fact from this remote land and whom one meets in Cairo more commonly come from Arabia Felix, which has frequent commercial relations with Abyssinians who have sufficient maritime skills to cross the gulf of the Red Sea. I met in Cairo some Abyssinian women who were virtually white: they were in all likelihood the descendants of several Portuguese families established in this country two centuries ago.

The Negroes who are brought from the kingdom of Darfur are most definitely black and are Negroes in the full sense of the word. Generally, they have a wide flat nose, thick upturned lips, and in sum a physiognomy displeasing to Europeans. Their moral qualities seemed to me to be in perfect accord with their physiognomy.

Finally, the Negroes who are brought from Fezzan are less black and distinguish themselves by their docility and intelligence. They are often marked by numerous fairly regular scars on their faces, which it is their custom to consider as an adornment.

The Negresses in general, although facing abject conditions, are not without ambition and a desire to please: as soon as they arrive in Cairo, they rub their bodies with grease or oil to better bring out the coloring of their skin. Although these women have in place of hair only a kind of wool, the custom of their country nevertheless leads them to make hundreds of little braids dipped, so to speak, in the butter or mutton fat. They all have their ears, and sometimes one or two nostrils, pierced to wear jewelry. I have even seen various women whose stomachs were covered with patterns of scars that never cease to amaze. While it may be true that these incisions are sometimes made because of an illness, I have good reason to believe that on other occasions they are made only for the pleasure of not having a plain stomach, which seems to me to be unfashionable among them.

MM. de Buffon and Valmont de Bomare report that the Ethiopians and several other peoples in Africa, as soon as their daughters are born, join by a kind of stitching those parts which nature has separated in them, and leave open only the necessary space for natural flows; that as the child grows, little by little the skin grows together so that it becomes necessary to separate it by an incision at the time of marriage.[11] It is even said that for this infibulation of the girls they use an asbestos thread because this material is not subject to decay. This opinion is generally believed no doubt because it was advanced by men who rightly enjoy a certain reputation.

The French found, in the house of the runaway Mamluks, Negresses who had become their concubines. They found some who had their natural parts almost completely removed; there is no doubt that this was the consequence of the stitching performed during their youth. I had recourse to various Negresses to discover more exactly how this supposed stitching was done and what were the motives that led them to do it. It did not take me long to confirm that this removal was nothing but the natural consequence of circumcision which seems among them as common for women as for men. Since the Mohammedan religion does not prescribe for women this operation, which was already practiced among the ancient Egyptians, and as it is still frequent today among the Copts, it is reasonable to infer that there are strong reasons for its perpetuation.[12]

It is a known fact that the labia majora often grow too long, especially in hot climates, and that the clitoris is severely oversized. Though neither the one or the other poses any obstacle to procreation, it seems however that a misshapen clitoris is considered by the Negroes as a disgusting deformity in that it gives the woman the appearance of being a man. This congenital deformity, though extremely rare among other nations, was well known among the ancients. Greek and Roman women at the time of the decay of morals were not ashamed to confess to this condition and simulated among themselves the pleasures which require the union of the two sexes. If we are to believe history, some of these women were driven by jealousy to acts of the greatest violence against these extraordinary lovers and punished their infidelities with death. The ancients depicted these illicit liaisons with the shades of the most horrible vice. Mr. Browne (L.C.) says that the operation performed among the Negroes is only an excision of the clitoris, already very precisely described by Aetius.[13] Nevertheless, according to all the information I have gathered, it seems very certain to me that, besides the clitoris, they cut off a part of the labia which they regard as superfluous. Immediately after this resection, which is done with a razor, they cover the wound with some substance made to absorb the blood flow which is normally not very heavy because they always take care to perform this operation at the age of one, two, four or six years. Sometimes it is even practiced at the age of six months. The remaining skin is then joined by means of a bandage on the thighs and another on the legs and the patient is thus kept lying down until the healing is complete. It is by this process that the cut flesh is joined together in such a way that gives rise to the belief that it was stitched in the girls' childhood.

If at the time of marriage the bridegroom finds the passage of the natural parts too narrow, a deft woman dilates it again with a razor, always being careful to make the opening smaller rather than larger for reasons that are easy to determine. Because of this precaution, when a newly married woman gives birth for the first time, a second incision is often necessary.

In certain cases female circumcision is repeated, especially when it is a case of checking the libertinism of an incorrigible woman. I do not know whether this remedy can be considered radical and I fear very much that if it were practiced in Europe it would be only a very weak palliative.

A lady of my acquaintance had for some years a beautiful Negresse aged about fifteen. This girl was, so her mistress was assured, "very well sewed up," and given this she was in no way afraid to leave the girl alone with men. Suddenly, the girl became pregnant without having undergone any operation other than that performed by a robust soldier.

As for the selling of Negroes, it resembles the selling of domestic animals in Europe. The buyer does a tour of the market, chooses what suits him the most. The *Ghellabi*, however much he may be exhorted, very rarely ventures to state the price he is asking for the individual in question, so that the buyer himself is forced to state how much he is willing to pay. If the offer is near the market price, the broker takes the right hands of the *Ghellabi* and the buyer. He then exhorts the first to agree to the sale while putting the other hand on the back of his neck to agree to the sale. All this is done accompanied by incredible noise and cries and looks more like an act of bondage or violence than one of mutual accord. The *Ghellabi* always answers "*eftahalla*,"[14] that is to say, "God will send me a better fortune," and if the offer is not increased by 5 to 10 piasters, there is little likelihood that a deal will be struck. Once the price is agreed upon, the noise stops suddenly. The broker, the *Ghellabi*, the buyer, and the purchased Negro or Negresse go to the office that is located at the exit of the *wikala*. There a Coptic scribe records that so and so bought from such and such a merchant a Negro of such an age and at such a price. He hands over a copy of this record to the buyer who pays at that moment a Spanish piaster to the proprietor of the *wikala*. The local people normally pay only a small deposit to the *Ghellabi* who accompanies the Negro to his new master. If in the course of the first twenty days a serious flaw is discovered in the Negroes or Negresses, such as that they snore a lot, wet their beds etc., they can be returned or exchanged. On the other hand, if the buyer is happy with the purchase, he pays the balance due on the agreed price. The French, more in a hurry to have Negresses at their disposal, and not in the least aware that such persons could be infected with venereal disease, did not think it necessary to observe this custom; it therefore resulted that several of them had to pay heavily for the pleasure which they enjoyed with them.

It is virtually impossible to say anything definitive about the cost of Negroes; it varies considerably and always in response to the frequency of the caravans, the number of Negroes that they bring, and sometimes also because of the number of Negroes who died of the plague. Nevertheless, since it is essential to say something about prices, I shall set forth as averages the following:

For a boy 10–14 years old	50–70 Spanish piasters
For a boy 15–18 years old	70–100 Spanish piasters
For a girl 8–12 years old	35–50 Spanish piasters
For a girl or woman 14–20 years old	70–90 Spanish piasters
For a eunuch 10–12 years old	160–200 Spanish piasters

I was at first astonished to see that the Negroes leave their travel companions, often a brother, sister, and even a mother, without showing the slightest regret. I had occasion, later, to convince myself that this is not due to any particular lack of sensitivity, but rather the hope of a better future makes them so. If later perchance they meet again, their joy is great and they pride themselves in mutual generosity.

There are some people who have formed so favorable an impression of the state of the Negroes sold in Cairo that they have considered the acquisition of Negroes there more like an adoption than enslavement. If, however, one defines slavery as the condition of a man who, by force or convention, has lost the ownership of his person and of whom a master can dispose of as his property, I would conclude that a Negro sold in Cairo is as much a slave as one sold in America, with the difference that his servitude is kinder in Egypt because he has to serve only one master. Consequently he is usually well fed and clothed and if he is well behaved, they may consider, after a number of years, finding him some sort of trade and marrying him off. If a Negro or Negresse on the other hand behaves poorly, or is found to be a thief, seriously negligent, impertinent, or guilty of amorous intrigues, etc., they are punished. It is often only by bastinado that they manage to correct them and to teach them something. When the owner of a Negro observes that he is incorrigible and that he is an unending source of trouble, he sends him off in his worst clothes to the market to be resold. There are always people to buy them in the belief that they will do better with them. Moreover, they are always sold for less than the newly arrived slaves.

Every year the Mamluks buy a relatively large number of Negroes for service in their homes; the males often became their comrades in arms and acceded with the passage of time, in addition to the Circassians or Georgians, to high places in their government. They are usually good soldiers.

For the rest, although the Negroes are better off in Egypt than among their own, love of country and the desire to return are not altogether unusual. But three daunting obstacles face them: lack of means, the long and difficult journey, and the excessive wickedness of the *Ghellabi*s who head the caravans. It would be interesting if one could explain satisfactorily why these people prefer to languish under a burning sky under a rod of iron in the most cruel enslavement, subject as much to the ferocity of men as to that of the animals which frequently prowl near their dwellings and which oblige them to be always on guard against them.

Of the Illnesses to which the Negroes are Subject upon Arrival in Cairo

Although the Negroes are normally healthy, strong, and robust, they are nevertheless subject to various diseases upon their arrival in Cairo, most of which are a natural outcome of their long and trying journey across the deserts and especially the result of the great climatic differences between Egypt and their land, always more or less part of the torrid zone. The main illness to which they are subject are the following:

1. Colds or afflictions of the respiratory tract. Given that the caravans normally arrive in Cairo in September when the nights are becoming cool and humid and that, in addition to their complete nudity, the Negroes are crammed at night into little rooms where they are constantly exposed alternately to hot and cold conditions, they frequently come down with colds. These by and large never have serious outcomes and always go away of their own.

2. Ophthalmia. Ophthalmia, which is endemic in Egypt, does not affect the Negroes as vehemently as it does the Europeans. It is difficult to determine in a satisfactory fashion the root causes of this disease. I have reviewed this subject in accordance with my findings in an appendix to a work that I propose to publish when circumstances permit.

3. Smallpox. This disease is often disastrous for the Negroes and *Ghellabi*s. It seems to be less widespread in the Sudan than in Egypt, but it is always deadly. The *Ghellabi*s maintain that smallpox never breaks out in their land except when the germ of infectious disease is brought

there. This assertion seems to be borne out by two observations. First, among the Negroes brought to Cairo, often two-thirds are found to have not yet suffered from this disease. Second, Doctor Poncé, who was sent for a century ago by the king of Abyssinia, notes in his travel report that his caravan had been stopped in Nubia to make sure that no one was suffering from smallpox.[15] When it was detected, it was customary to subject the caravan to a quarantine. I have gathered information from numerous persons in order to determine whether this practice still persists. But no one was able to give me satisfactory information in this regard.

Smallpox is generally widespread among the Negroes. The onset of the disease is often accompanied by more complications than among whites, in all likelihood because Negroes have thicker and denser skin. The fever that proceeds the onset of the disease is often very high. Unless one has already observed this disease several times among the Negroes, it is difficult for a European doctor to diagnose it as such, unless concomitant symptoms or a broader epidemic point to the nature of the disease. The little spots which manifest themselves at the time of the outbreak are all the more ambiguous because one cannot detect any nuance of white or red. The color of the skin and the spots is identical. Moreover, since the new arrivals are subject to a skin disease, of which I will speak later, and are often covered with spots, the result of mosquito bites, the doctor finds himself facing doubts about the real nature of the disease. It is likely that the *Ghellabis* would lose fewer Negroes if they attended to them a little, and especially if they were willing to consult a European doctor. But either they cannot grasp this reality or they are not in the least disposed to allow for any such expense.

4. A skin disease that the inhabitants of Cairo call in slang *aesch el medina*.[16] It is almost universal among the new arrivals. This disease has been frequently confused with scabies either because of the shape of the pustule or the severe itch that it causes. If nevertheless one deems the disease not to be contagious and given that scabies is relatively rare in Egypt, one is easily convinced that the people of the country are correct to call the disease by the special name of *aesch el medina*, or bread of the city, to point to the fact that this is the most common disease among the new arrivals from the Sudan. The disease manifests itself in stages—a number of little spots, somewhat pointed, more or less plentiful on all

parts of the body without fever or any other irritation. Sometimes a full rash with these spots happens rapidly and in a few days. Sometimes its takes place slowly and lasts several weeks. Sometimes also it remains stable and looks exactly like dry scabies (*scabies sicca*). On other occasions, the spots grow and one observes a purely serous or purulent substance always accompanied day and night by a severe itch. I have observed several cases where the spots were so numerous that both the upper and lower extremities were swollen as if with smallpox. It is not unusual to observe a more or less considerable fever.

I have absolutely no idea of the real causes of this disease. Some people would maintain that it is chiefly caused by a change in nutrition, especially by the habit of eating meat. But this assertion is absolutely false because I often found at the slave market many individuals on whom this disease was already visible and thus at a time when they were still following the diet of their land.

Left to follow its course, the disease sometimes lasts several months and even becomes deforming. If, on the other hand, after a full rash breaks out one uses the remedies that I will talk about, the disease disappears in a relatively short time. In keeping with my observation of the inhabitants of the country, the most used and effective method of curing this disease is to rub the patient every two days, especially his body, with what they call *kiske*.[17] It is a semi-cooked, dried, ground yeast which is mixed for several days with milk and then exposed to the sun in order for the mixture to dry out. The rubbing with this ointment must continue until the rash completely disappears, which happens within a week or at most two weeks.

I have also seen used with success the following remedy: one moistens a portion of lupine flour with a good dose of lemon juice then one applies this mixture to the body of the patient. He is then exposed in this state to the sun for several hours. When the mixture has completely dried out on the skin, the patient is taken to a steambath. The application of this ointment must be repeated every two days until the complete disappearance of the symptoms.

I have also seen used with equal success a liniment made of flax oil, sulfur, and nut-gall. No internal medicine is ever used in the treatment of this illness. Those who have tried to use mercury and sulfur did so with no visible success.

It is wise to give only very few fatty foods to the newly arrived Negroes, whether they are ill or not. The people of the land even maintain that for the first forty days they should be given only rice, bread, and plain vegetables. While it is to be expected that these people can only become accustomed gradually to a way of life so opposed to their own, I nevertheless have found that one could without danger cut back on the number of days.

5. Diarrhea and Dysentery. These illnesses are formidable for all newly arrived people in Egypt. There are two principal ways of safeguarding oneself against them. The first consists of a careful diet, that is to say eating little meat. The second is to dress warmly as winter nears. As for the rest, since my observations on the nature and treatment of dysentery are very numerous, I am saving them in their entirety for a study of the medical topography of Cairo.

6. The Plague. Not only Negroes newly-arrived in Cairo, but also those who have lived in this capital for several years, very easily succumb to this fatal infectious disease. It is, in my opinion, extremely difficult to account for this particular susceptibility. All that can be said about adjustment to a new environment and about a particular inclination of the humors to contract this disease is very vague and conjectural. I will endeavor also to expound upon this subject with special concern when I publish my findings on the plague.

7. The Guinea Worm, the Dragon, or the Scourge of Medina, (*Furia infernalis, Vena Medinensis, Dracunculum, Gordius Medinensis, Dragontia Aeginetae*). Apparently there is in the waters of the Sudan, and may be in those that one finds in the desert, a sort of worm that penetrates the skin, mainly through the lower regions of the body. It is about as thick as a violin string, sometimes even finer, pointed at both ends like an earthworm, and is as long as four to six feet. One detects its presence owing to its twisting under the skin, which makes it look very much like little varicose veins. Sometimes it stays put for a long time without causing any discomfort or without even being detected. But once it has reached full grown size, it causes inflammation which leads every time to suppuration. Once the abscess opens, the worm comes out head first. Individuals who harbor this worm in whatever part of their body often die of exhaustion, if they do not seek timely treatment.[18]

There are in Cairo some Negroes who have made a name for themselves for knowing how to extract skillfully this worm. For if the worm is broken, it is dangerous for the patient. The Negroes try to seize one end of the worm which they wrap around a piece of wood and which they tape to the limb. Every day or every two days, they wrap a further part of the worm around the stick in a manner such that in the end with the requisite patience, they extract the worm completely. The rest of the procedure requires nothing but dealing with a simple sore. According to observations made on the extraction of this worm in Europe, if one blows tobacco smoke into the sore, the worm dies. The same outcome can be had by placing a bandage with mercury over it. Dr. Loeffler reports successful treatment with an ammonia liniment, which lessens the pain and dissipates the inflammation.

8. Venereal disease. The Negroes often bring this disease from their country. Diagnosis is sometimes difficult. Consequently, it is wise to warn those who buy a Negresse that having relations with her is not without possible dangerous consequences.

Frambosia or yaws, which kills so many Negroes in America, is completely unknown in Egypt.

Notes

I wish to thank Professor Bernard Lewis who brought this text to my attention and suggested that I translate it. In addition to providing me with the text, Professor Lewis also furnished me with a draft translation of a good portion of it. It goes without saying that I am nevertheless entirely responsible for any errors in the final version. It should be noted that I have followed Frank's text as regards transliteration and capitalization. At times it is inconsistent. The notes explain the origins of certain Arabic terms and colloquialisms.

1. Paris: Migneret and Brigithe Mathé, 1802. The brief biography that follows is drawn largely from *Le dictionnaire de biographie française* (Paris: Libraire LeTouzey et Ané, 1979), 14: 1097–1098.

2. William George Browne (1768–1813) was the author of *A Journey to Darfur* in John Pinkerton, ed., *A General Collection of the Best and Most Interesting Voyages and Travels*, vol. 15 (London, 1814).

3. Frank refers throughout the text to the "Ghellabis," a word which appears to be a Sudanese colloquial term used to describe the slave dealers. It is evidently derived from an adjectival form or *nisba* of the word *ghallāb*, which in Arabic means victor or conqueror.

4. The term which Frank renders as "*al-Habirri*" is derived from the Arabic word *ḥabr*, *ḥibr*, pl. *aḥbār* which in medieval or classical Arabic was used to designate an "authority" or "scribe", often a non-Muslim. Again the *nisba* ending seems to be employed in this colloquial rendition and usage, hence *ḥabrī*.

5. The correct Arabic transliteration is *dhura* which refers to various kinds of sorghum, millet, and wheat depending on the context or adjective modifying it.

6. "Cortbache" is Frank's rendition of *kurbāj*, *karābīj*.

7. This seventeenth-century Italian travel account was published in France as *Voyages de Pietro della Valle,...dans la Turquie, l'Égypte, la Palestine, la Perse, les Indes orientales et autres lieux*, trans. Étienne Carneau and François Le Comte (Rouen: R. Machuel, 1745), 8 vols.

8. Bornu—the region and state on the southwest shore of Lake Chad—was an important supplier of slaves to the Fezzan and the Qaramanli dynasty (r. 1711–1835) based in Tripoli. For a detailed account of late eighteenth-century and nineteenth-century Bornu, see Louis Brenner, *The Shehus of Kukawa: A History of the al-Kanemi Dynasty of Bornu* (Oxford: Clarendon Press, 1973). "Havnia" is not a recognized geographic designation. Assuming that Frank was consulting a primitive European map of Africa, the region in question may well have been "Hausa" with its capital in Kano. For a broad overview of trade between the Sudan and Egypt, see Terence Walz, *Trade Between Egypt and Bilad al-Sudan, 1700–1820* (Cairo: IFAO, 1978).

9. For a thorough statistical survey of the number of African slaves imported to the Mediterranean world, see Ralph Austen, "The Mediterranean Islamic Slave Trade Out of Africa: Towards a Census," in *The Human Commodity: Perspectives on the trans-Saharan Slave Trade*, ed. by Elizabeth Savage (London: Frank and Cass, 1992), see especially the table on p. 227.

10. Year six of the French Republican calendar, adopted in 1792, corresponds to the common era year 1798.

11. Georges Louis Leclerc comte de Buffon (1707–1788) and Jacques Christophe Valmont de Bomare (1731–1807) did not coauthor a book as might be assumed from what Frank says. Buffon was a prolific naturalist who wrote dozens of works on animal and plant life, medicine, and the like. Frank could have drawn his information from any of Buffon's many works. Valmont de Bomare was, on the other hand, more restrained in his output. In all likelihood, Frank was drawing on his *Dictionnaire raisonné universel d'histoire naturelle...* (Paris: Didot-le-Jeune, 1764), 5 vols.

12. For a further perspective on this question, see Jonathan P. Berkey, "Circumcision Circumscribed: Female Excision and Cultural Accommodation in the Medieval Near East," *International Journal of Middle East Studies* 28 (1996): 19–38.

13. The Greek physician Aetios of Amida (Diyarbakır in modern Turkey) lived in the sixth century C.E. and was an active author ca. 530–560. For the original Greek text, see *Gynaekologie des Aetios* (Leipzig: Fock, 1901). The text is book sixteen of his *Biblia Iatrika Hekskaideka.*

14. Assuming that Frank's translation is correct, the precise grammatical form rendered here as "Eftahalla" is not entirely clear. Perhaps Frank heard "iftaḥ yā allāh—that is literally "open" or "bestow (on me a profit) Oh God", perhaps a colloquialism. Otherwise the only other possible phrase would be "astaghifru'llāh," literally I seek God's pardon, a phrase used in polite conversation to decline a compliment or offer. But this meaning does not correspond with Frank's translation.

15. The author and possible title of the work remain uncertain. The catalogue of the Bibliothèque Nationale does not contain any reference to a Doctor Poncé who traveled to Abyssinia in the early eighteenth century.

16. "ʿAysh," meaning "life" in Arabic, is used in colloquial Cairene Arabic to mean bread. The diphthong is often omitted and instead the word is pronounced as "ʿīsh".

17. The Arabic word properly transliterated as "kishk" refers to a variety of flour and milk mixtures that are dried in the sun and used as a base for soups.

18. Guinea worm, a parasite of the class of nematode worm or round worm, is commonly found in India and parts of Africa. It is not to be confused with another parasitic worm found in the irrigation canals of the Nile that causes the fatal disease known as "bilharziasis". The latter was first diagnosed in Western medicine by the German physician Theodor Bilharz (d. 1862).

The Mamluks: The Mainstay of Islam's Military Might

DAVID AYALON

The importance and purport of the Mamluk phenomenon has been misunderstood for various reasons. The study of Islam and its history is still in its infancy. The amount of the source material is immense, and the number of those who tackle it is relatively small. The military, and even more so the socio-military, subject long occupied quite a low place in the Islamicists' scale of preferences, in spite of its significance. Also, the Mamluk system is a phenomenon that has no real parallel outside Islamic civilization. Furthermore, slave rulers are not to the liking of many people.

When, as a student, I started studying the Mamluks, I was told by a prominent Islamicist that working on such a subject is similar in importance to working on the history of the Fiji Islands. No wonder, therefore, that the scholarly image of the Mamluks was, on the whole, with but a few important exceptions, negative and fragmentary. The real picture, in my view, which I came to see only very slowly, is completely different.

In a few words it can be said that the Mamluks were the determining military factor in Islam during the greatest part of its existence, both offensively and defensively. Without that factor Islam's geographical boundaries would have been much narrower. As for the struggle between Islam and Christian Europe, with its ever-growing technological preponderance, it must be pointed out in the clearest possible terms that on sea the Muslims ceased to be a world factor as early as the eleventh century. On land the same result was postponed for a good number of centuries, mainly owing to the military might of the Mamluk system and its offshoots.

> Mamluk—the literal meaning: owned, acquired; the meaning in practice: a) slave; b) gradually confined to a fair-skinned slave horseman.

The Mamluk institution, which lasted for a thousand years—from the first half of the ninth century to the first half of the nineteenth—formed, on the one hand, part and parcel of the Muslim slave system, the roots of which go back to the pre-Islamic period. It was a moderate kind of slavery. On the other hand, it formed a very special category within that system. The Mamluks can be classified as slaves who became masters and belonged to the uppermost layer of Muslim military society. Their overwhelming majority was brought over to the Muslim world from countries situated beyond its borders, which means that they were born infidels. For a long period their countries of origin were in Central Asia and its neighboring areas. This implies that they were fair-skinned pagans. Blacks could not form part of the Muslim military elite.

The Mamluks, who were brought by slave merchants, belonged mainly to tribal societies, distinguished by their superb military qualities as cavalrymen. Only the very best of them were chosen, after a strict selection. They were taken from their homelands at or near the age of puberty. When they reached their Muslim destination (usually the court of a ruler or an important military commander) they were converted to Islam. They were first taught the basic tenets of Islam, and later received the best military training of the time. This was, of course, cavalry training. When the Mamluk terminated the period of Islamic studies and military training, he was usually manumitted.

The important point relating to the Mamluk's manumission was that in Islam the real and lasting loyalty between patron and slave started after the slave was freed. The patron and his Mamluk freedmen were a kind of a big "family," in which the Mamluk was bound by strong links of loyalty to his patron manumittor on the one hand, and to his comrades in slavery and manumission on the other. These ties existed and were fostered within the framework of an exceptionally strong awareness of Islam's absolute superiority over any other religion, be it monotheistic or pagan.

In addition to all these characteristics there was yet another unique one, typifying the Mamluk institution, without which all the others would have lost their main importance. This was an institution of one-generation nobility. The sons of the Mamluks were ousted from it, for two reasons. First, in the environment of ease and comfort into which they were born and in which they grew up, those sons could not preserve the military qualities of their parents acquired in the harsh conditions of their homeland. Second, their influential Mamluk fathers could intervene on their behalf, and unduly accelerate their advancement. The ousting of the sons was facilitated by the fact that they were given Arab-Muslim names whereas their fathers bore Turkish ones. All this meant that the Mamluk system had to be fed by a constant stream of fresh recruits arriving from their countries of origin.

The slave trade, and especially its Mamluk component, could be conducted regularly and over a very long period, because it was, generally speaking, beneficial to most parties concerned, including, quite often, the families of the enslaved boys. For those boys it was a great change for the better in their standard of living, and many of them were destined to make brilliant careers.

This system also had serious drawbacks. The Mamluk-importing countries did not have direct control over the sources of Mamluk supply, and those nearer the sources had a big advantage over those situated further away. The prices of the Mamluks were very high, and the patron had to spend additional money on them and wait long years before they became full-fledged soldiers. The loyalty which the Mamluk owed to his patron on the one hand, and to Islam on the other, sometimes clashed. For reasons I cannot enumerate here, the sources of the importation of pagan Mamluks possessing the proper warrior qualities were depleted and could not be substituted in a nearby area. Finally, Mamluk rule and economic prosperity did not necessarily go together.

Under such conditions of the depletion of the pagan sources, the recruitment of Christian Mamluks (Greeks, Armenians, and others) was inevitable. That process was gradual, and reached its peak in the Ottoman

Empire, the picked army of which was a direct offshoot of the socio-military Mamluk system. How vital was the continuation of that system can be learned from the following fact. Enslaving Christian inhabitants of the lands of Islam was forbidden by Muslim law. Yet there were important Muslim rulers, and not only the Ottomans, who seem to have violated it. The recruitment of Christians helped to solve some difficult problems: the Ottomans had full control of their Mamluk sources of supply. And, what is at least as important, it was much easier to adapt those Mamluks to technological progress than it was in the case of their pagan counterparts. This difference in adaptation applies not only to the purely military field, but beyond it as well.

That the Mamluks formed the mainstay of Islam's military might is supported by overwhelming evidence in the Muslim sources. At this juncture I shall confine myself to one outstanding example. Ibn Khaldūn (d. 1406), the greatest Muslim historian-sociologist, gave a detailed account of the Mamluk phenomenon from its inception and up to his own time. There he stated, inter alia, that the Mamluks were the saviors of Islam when it was breathing its last breath (*iḥyā᾽ ramaqihi*). This evidence of Ibn Khaldūn completely escaped the notice of the Islamicists for two reasons: because it is included in his chronicle, and not in his much better known *Prolegomena* (*al-Muqaddima*) to that chronicle; and because of insufficient awareness of the centrality of the Mamluk system. As for the value of that evidence, I believe that only a few passages in the *Prolegomena* equal it in importance. In the same account Ibn Khaldūn states that out of the superb human military material that serves as a source for the acquisition of Mamluks only the very best were selected (*iṣṭifā᾽ al-ʿilya minhum*). The sieving was so strict, that what was left for the final choice was: "The boys like golden dinars and the girls like pearls" (*al-ghilmān k'al-danānīr w'al-jawārī k'al-la᾽ālī᾽*). The important feminine aspect of the Mamluk phenomenon will not be dealt with here.

It was quite foreseeable that the wrong image of the Mamluks would find its way to quite a few of the members of the Arab intelligentsia (Arab Islamicists think otherwise today). The most outstanding example is the book by the late president of Egypt, Gamal Abd el-Nasser, *The Philosophy of the Revolution*, read by many millions in its Arabic original and in numerous translations. Among the foreigners who sucked the marrow of Egypt and caused its decline, Nasser enumerates the Mamluks as major contributors. In 1954, in connection with the British evacuation of the Suez Canal, the London *Observer* decided to give Nasser a most impressive buildup, and published his book in installments. I was then in London, and sent the *Observer* an article, the main purpose of which was to refute Nasser's accusations against the Mamluks. I relied there also on Ibn Khaldūn's evidence. The editors of that paper rejected it with amusingly unconvincing arguments.

Sure enough, one can also find in the Muslim sources criticisms of the phenomenon of slave becoming master in the spirit of the saying: "when a slave reigns," but criticisms of this kind did not have the slightest effect on the Mamluks' standing and functioning, although they always looked for acceptance and popularity among their subjects. Obviously, the system had its faults, some of them grave. Some of its immediate and long range deficiencies are discussed below.

In this connection it would be worthwhile to mention the admiring words of Napoleon Bonaparte and his officers about the superb military qualities of the Mamluks. This evidence, from the turn of the nineteenth century, is important for the following reasons. The French land army was at that time the best in the world. The pick of that army, headed by one of the greatest commanders in human history, and by a group of superb officers, was sent in 1798 to conquer Egypt. The adversaries of the French, the Mamluks, by contrast, formed at that time an absolutely anachronistic military body, on the verge of its total extinction. In spite of all that, members of the French high command discerned the Mamluks' unique military ability. In 1799, for example, Napoleon stated that five Mamluks would, in close combat, beat six or seven dragoons. But, as they lacked drill and order, a French squadron of horse would discomfit five hundred Mamluks.

In order to place the Mamluks in their proper Muslim context, one must review Islam's frontiers with the rest of the world. The Muslim World, "The Abode of Islam" (*Dār al-Islām*), had four main fronts with the non-Muslim world, all of which had been included under the name of "Abode of War" (*Dār al-ḥārb*). One of them was monotheistic, and the other three pagan, or mainly pagan (this applies to the period following the first great thrust of the Muslim conquests). The first was the Christian front, most of which was European, with the exception of Byzantine Anatolia. The second was the African front—pagan, with the exception of its Nubian-Christian section. The third, the Indian front, was pagan. The fourth, the Eurasian (European-Asiatic) front, was pagan (with temporary Christian and Jewish islands), stretching from Afghanistan to the Black Sea, with its heart in Central Asia (and particularly Transoxania—"The Land Beyond the River," *Mā Warāʾ al-Nahr*[1]—with its two main towns Bukhara and Samarqand).

Each of the four fronts will be discussed here, from the point of view of their serving as a source of military manpower for Islam, or otherwise. The fronts of decisive importance in Islam were the first and the fourth, both of which will be the last to be discussed in this paper. The first was considered extremely negative by the Muslims, and the fourth extremely positive. In the very long run the positive one weakened gradually, whereas the negative became stronger. This growing imbalance between the two fronts had far-reaching consequences, which are felt up to the present day.

The Indian and the African Fronts

About the two secondary pagan fronts, I will say the following. India, in spite of its immense population, served as only a minor source for the importation of Mamluks. Following the great Muslim conquests in India, in the first half of the eleventh century, the Ghaznawid conquerors, whose capital was in Afghanistan, formed Indian Mamluk units. But the recruitment of Mamluks from that source was short-lived, and did not spread westwards. The importation of slaves other than Mamluks from India did exist, but it does not seem to have been on a large scale, and certainly did not go far beyond Indian territory (with the exception of Indian eunuchs). Another significant characteristic typifying that front was that, whereas it had been the constant target of Muslim invasions for many centuries, it never threatened the lands of Islam with a counterinvasion, neither did it serve as a noticeable source of migrations of free people, be they groups or individuals, into those lands. This means that the number of pagan Indians who entered Muslim territory, settled there, and consequently adopted Islam, was not considerable (the Islamization of Indians as a result of Muslim expansion into their own territory is, of course, another matter).

As for the blacks of Africa, they, like the Indians, did not seriously threaten the Abode of Islam by invasion from their countries of origin. Unlike them, they could not become Mamluks under any conditions (the rise of black eunuchs inside and outside Mamluk society belongs to a different category). Yet, their contribution to Islam's might was very great, particularly as slaves serving in the infantry. It is, however, very difficult to have a full picture of that great contribution, because of the more than relative anonymity of those armies, including that of their black commanders, especially in the major centers of Islam's military strength. Many a time the presence of black armies, in the field or elsewhere, was revealed by complete accident. Even when the black element of the army was very strong and its presence most conspicuous, as, for example, in the reigns of the Tulunids, the Ikhshidids, and the Fatimids of Egypt, it is not at all easy for the historian to give a picture of its internal structure and functioning, because of the way it is mentioned in the sources. It was Saladin who, in the second half of the twelfth century, administered a severe blow to the black armies, because they had been a mainstay of the Fatimid Shiʿites in their struggle against the Ayyubid Sunnites for the dominance of Egypt. Thenceforward the blacks did not constitute a significant military factor in those major centers.

Speaking of the blacks, one should bear in mind that they, exactly like the Mamluks, were part and parcel of the Muslim slave institution. This shows how overwhelming was the contribution of that institution to Muslim military strength. The rulers who, for geographical and economic reasons, had to recruit mainly blacks for their slave armies, were those of the Arab peninsula (in which such armies already existed before the advent of Islam) and of North Africa. There one also finds black cavalry units. The Mamluks, however, were much more valued than the blacks in those countries (cp. the armies of the Ayyubids and the Rasulids in Arabia, and the Mamluk contingent which Saladin sent to fight in North Africa).[2]

The Eurasian Front

The great story of Islam, and the most positive from its point of view, was the fourth front, which stretched from Central Asia along Islam's northeastern and northern borders and beyond, and which was inhabited mainly by the Turkish and other nomads akin to them, and also by other ethnic groups.[3] This was a huge human reservoir, which, admittedly, was not as big as the Indian one, but which far exceeded numerically that of the Arabian peninsula.

It was most fortunate for Islam that the Arabs, already in their earlier conquering thrusts, reached that front, and more precisely, its vital section for Islam—Transoxania. The people of that region, which attained a high level of civilization and was very rich, put up a particularly stubborn resistance to the Muslim attacks over a considerable period of time. But when Transoxania was finally conquered, its Islamized population developed a very strong Muslim awareness, and eagerness to take part in the holy war (*jihād*). It fostered strong ties with the heart of the Muslim world, mainly by means of the yearly pilgrimage to Mecca and Medina, and, according to al-Muqaddasī, of the second half of the tenth century, the command of that population of classical Arabic was better than that of some of the Arabic-speaking people. They primarily adopted Sunnī Islam, and especially its Hanafite version.

At this point it is very important to remember that well before the final conquest of Transoxania, the center of gravity of Islam's military strength moved northeastward from Syria in the direction of Khorasan in Eastern Iran. Arabs, who underwent a far-reaching process of Iranization, as well as pure Khorasani Iranians, brought about the annihilation of the Umayyads and their replacement by the ʿAbbasids, who, shortly after they came to power, moved Islam's capital eastward from Damascus to Baghdad. It was they who, with their Khorasani armies, later conquered Transoxania. Thus, the Eastern Iranian context relating to the entrance of Mamluks and other pagans to the lands of Islam through Transoxania is of supreme importance.

Throughout the ages Mamluks entered the Muslim countries not only through Transoxania, but through a much longer frontier (the main inlet of Mamluks moved steadily westward). But during the first centuries of the existence of the Mamluk institution, which were the essential ones in its formation, their main entrance corridor was that "Land Beyond the River," and the Land of Khwarizm adjacent to it. Through that same corridor entered the Seljuks and their Turcomans from the end of the tenth century onward, and after them the Mongols during the thirteenth century. The Islam which all those met when they first set foot on Muslim soil was, generally speaking, Sunnī,[4] mainly Hanafī, and this appears to have left a very deep impression. The Turkish Mamluks, who formed their spearhead, are said by the tenth century geographers al-Istakhrī and Ibn Hawqal to have filled Transoxania with the surplus overflowing westwards. They were also considered by them to have been unequaled warriors. That situation created ideal conditions for implanting a powerful Islamic consciousness and fostering a holy war spirit in those Mamluks.

This leads us to the strong links connecting the two other elements with the Mamluks. Islam was exposed to invasion (or penetration) on a large scale from only two fronts: the first, a monotheistic one, and the fourth, a Eurasian, mainly pagan, one. The possibility of a similar exposure from India or black Africa was marginal at best, as already stated. The singularity of the fourth front was that those who entered the lands of Islam through Eurasia, whether by invasion, penetration, or otherwise, eventually adopted the Muslim religion. The Seljuks adopted Islam immediately, on the verge of their penetration, and the Mongols ultimately followed the same course. Furthermore, the Mongols greatly fostered the spread of Islam far outside pre-Mongol boundaries: in Southern Russia (the Mongol Khanate of the Golden Horde) and from Central Asia to areas stretching well beyond it. It goes without saying that the Mamluks, brought over individually and at a very young age, had all, without exception, adopted Islam.

Such a development on the first, the monotheistic, front was absolutely impossible. It was unthinkable that a victorious Christian ruler conquering a Muslim territory would, together with his army and people, convert to Islam. It was equally unimaginable that a Christian ruler or commander would do what the Seljuks had done, namely adopt Islam just before entering Muslim territory; and that, in the wake of his advance in that territory, numerous Islamized Christians would leave their homelands and join him, as did the multitudes of pagan Turcomans, who continued to flow into Transoxania, Iran, and beyond in the footsteps of the Seljuk dynasty.[5]

The basic difference between the two fronts is also apparent in their respective attitudes toward prisoners of war. Christian prisoners adopting Islam after the relative stabilization of the first front were not a usual phenomenon. First of all, it was quite difficult to convince them that Islamic monotheism might be superior to theirs. Secondly, within the boundaries of Islam, the local Christians enjoyed the status of a tolerated community, which could only encourage the Christian prisoners to stick to their religion. Thirdly, and no less important, between the Muslims and the Byzantines an institution of the exchange of prisoners came into being, the like of which does not seem to have existed before in dimension and durability. Thus the Christian prisoners could cherish the quite realistic hope that one day they would return to their Christian homeland.

The fourth front posed a fundamentally different situation, for the following reasons. First, it was far easier to convert the numerous prisoners of war of that front from their pagan religion to Islam. Second, there were no pagan communities within the boundaries of Islam, because pagans did not have the right to exist there. (The Zoroastrians, and in a different way the Hindus, formed a special case.) Third, there was barely a trace of a stable institution of the exchange of prisoners on that front. The overwhelming majority of the prisoners was bound to convert to Islam.

Let us return to the three elements we mentioned earlier. The Muslims justifiably considered the Mamluks, the Turks, and the Mongols, all of whom came from the same direction, and through the same corridor, as belonging to the same stock. The most common word used for the Mamluk is Turk (pl. *atrāk*). The dominant name of the Mamluk Sultanate was "The State of the Turks" (*dawlat al-turk*, or *al-atrāk*). The Turks of the Seljuks were certainly Turk (or Turkman), and the Mongols were considered to be "a kind of Turk" (*nawʾ min al-turk*). In the course of time the names Turk and Tatar became fully synonymous. In the famous battle of ʿAyn Jalut (in the valley of Jezreet) in 1260, where the Turkish Mamluks defeated the Mongols, the contemporary historian Abū Shāma emphasized the fact that the two adversaries were of the same stock or race (*min jins wāḥid*). Since practically all the Mamluks were born as unbelievers in the lands of heathendom, what is implied in what had previously been said is that in that important battle the infidels of yesterday vanquished the Muslims of tomorrow.[6]

No comparable state of affairs could arise on any of the other three fronts. However, in spite of all the assumptions in the Arabic sources about the common origin and similar background of the peoples coming from the fourth front, there existed an almost impenetrable barrier separating the Mamluks from all the others, including the Turks and the Mongols. One could belong to the Mamluk socio-military body only if one passed through the course of slavery and (usually) manumission described in the short summary of the Mamluk system at the opening of this article. Within the army the non-Mamluks, whatever their origin, were allowed to serve only in auxiliary forces. A very limited and brief attempt to include Mongol freedmen in the selected Mamluk units of the Mamluk Sultanate during the first decades of its existence (the second half of the thirteenth century) was not continued, in spite of the great admiration of the Mongols prevailing among the Mamluks. The extent to which Mongol institutions influenced those of the Mamluks is a question in need of further study. Whatever the case may be, the quite common belief, which I long shared, namely, that the Mamluks were judged among themselves according to the laws of the Great Yasa of Chingiz Khan, proved to be both wrong and unreasonable, as I think I did show in a previous detailed study.[7] The Mamluk element was the decisive and leading one, whereas the two other elements complemented and usually supported it.

In this connection it should be emphasized that within the wide boundaries of the whole Muslim world there was no armed power that could threaten the Mamluk military preponderance, to say nothing of replacing it. That formidable fact became evident as soon as the Mamluk army came into being. The Khorasani army of northeastern Iran, which was composed of free men, and which replaced the Arab army, also composed of free men, tried in vain, together with its offshoots, to oppose its successor, the Mamluk army, and finally disappeared. With the appearance of the Mamluks as the major Muslim military power in the first half of the ninth century, the Mamluk army was accompanied by units of free men from Transoxania (Ferghanis, Ushrusis, and others), namely, from the regions from which the Mamluks themselves were recruited, or from their near vicinity. These too disappeared after a certain period. Such was the long history of the Mamluks.

At this juncture it should be stated most emphatically that Caliph al-Muʿtaṣim (833–842), who made the Mamluks the mainstay of ʿAbbasid might, decided to build Samarra and move the capital from Baghdad, first and foremost because he wanted to get rid of the antagonism of the more veteran units to those Mamluks and mold his new army according to his own lights. All other reasons were marginal to this one. Samarra ceased to be the capital just after half a century, but the Mamluks came to stay as Islam's main offensive and defensive instrument. The great drawback of the Mamluk regiment of al-Muʿtaṣim was that it came into being when the dismemberment of the Caliphate was already underway. Thus the Mamluks were not used on the frontier of Islam as part of a general policy. It was the successor states that made use of the Mamluks within the framework of much narrower targets.

Let us return once again to our three elements. The contribution of the Mamluks in the East was a deep penetration from Transoxania to other parts of Central Asia and beyond from the ninth century onward (by the Samanids and their Mamluks) and the great conquests of Indian territory from Afghanistan in the first half of the eleventh century (by the Ghaznawids and their Mamluks), which formed the decisive Muslim push into India, and which laid the major basis for Islam in that sub-continent. In the West, it was a Mamluk contingent of the Seljuks that gave the coup de grâce (in 1060) to the Shiʿite pro-Fatimid rebellion near Kufa in Southern Iraq, thus curbing the Shiʿite expansion in the East. And what is far more important: the Mamluks were the decisive factor in the Seljuk great victory of Manzikert (north of Lake Van) in 1071.[8] That victory, as is so well known, opened Anatolia to Islamic dominance, thus paving the way for the birth and rise of the Ottoman Empire, a successor state of the Seljuk empire, and a Mamluk state of a special brand. This already gives us an idea of the immense role played by the Mamluks in the first front, to be discussed later.

As for the role of the Turcomans (*turkmān*, to distinguish them from the Mamluk *atrāk*), their chances of advancing westward without the victories of the Mamluks would have greatly diminished. However, as an auxiliary army, their contribution was both important and essential.

Furthermore, they were numerous, and, being nomads, they spread over wide areas. The Mamluks, by contrast, were relatively few, and were stationed mainly in the big urban centers (they always formed a quite small nucleus of the Muslim ruler's army, and were town dwellers). Because the Turcomans were so widespread, Turkish became the dominant language in Azerbaijan, Anatolia, parts of Southern Iran, and, for a time, even in Northern Syria. In all probability, the Turcomans accelerated the spread of Islam, especially in Anatolia. The enormous contribution of the Mongols to the spread of Islam has already been mentioned.

In a linguistic context it would be worthwhile to point out that the origin of the three major languages of Islam (Arabic, Persian, and Turkish), all of which are written in the Arab script, was in the East, in an area stretching from the Arab Peninsula to the northeast, and the homeland of two of those three is situated on the two sides of the front we are now considering. Each of them penetrates the territorial boundaries of the other, and to a certain extent competes with the other. One should also bear in mind the great impact of Persian on the languages spoken in the conquered and Islamized territories in the East, especially India. By contrast, along the first front (the Christian, monotheistic one), there was no similar affinity of language or script.[9] And I would say that a thrust of any language from beyond that front into the lands of Islam, as happened with the mighty and deep thrust of Turkish from the opposite front, cannot be considered even hypothetically. Thus, to the religious barrier in that front the barriers of language and script were added, which could only intensify the alienation between Islam and its neighboring Christianity. After the Crusades, which caused the thickening of the barrier, especially from the Muslim side, a well known Muslim historian, Ibn Taghribirdi (d. 1470), had this to say about the Franks, while enumerating the names of the world rulers and their countries in 1457:

> As for the kingdoms of the Franks, they are sixteen kingdoms. The nearest of all them to the shores of the country of Egypt is the island of Cyprus. Its ruler to day is Jawan the son of Jinus the son of Jak the son of Bidu, the son of Antun the son of Jinus. As for the rest of their kings and their lands it is difficult to mention their names, because of the out-

> landishness of their form. One has to spell correctly each letter of those names to facilitate reading them. This would require a long explanation which would serve no purpose.[10]

Thus, of all the formidable and frightening lands of the West, the only one worthy of note was the small island of Cyprus, because, since the twenties of the fifteenth century onwards, it was a tributary of Mamluk Sultanate!

As a result of all the developments described above, a considerable part of the fourth front was integrated into the lands of Islam. Consequently, the section from which Mamluks could be recruited was narrowed. In the first front, the state of things differed fundamentally . The struggle on sea had already been decided, while on land the difficulties for Islam had been increasing and accumulating, because of the growing technological preponderance of the adversary.

The Christian European Front

We arrive now at the front that had been the most difficult and dangerous to the Muslims, and in which they had been the ultimate losers. Defeat took place in two stages separated by a long period. The first stage was on sea, the second on land. Before dealing with these two stages, it should be pointed out that since the advent of Islam, the dominant struggle was between the two monotheistic religions, with their enormous dynamism and with the determined aim of each to convert the whole world to its version of monotheism.

For many centuries the heart and core of that struggle was the Mediterranean basin, where its outcome was primarily decided. Fernand Braudel, in his well known book *La Mediterranée et le Monde Mediterrané*, rightly stresses the great importance of factors of *longue durée*, but he does not attribute sufficient weight to the long and persistent human struggle with which we deal here. More than half of the length of the Mediterranean coastal area is inhabited by Muslims, which remained true even after the conquest of the Iberian Peninsula by the Christians. Braudel had a very superficial knowledge of Islam, its history, and its character.

The struggle on sea was decided already during the eleventh century. It basically spelled the end of the history of Islam as a naval world power. This fundamental transformation of the Mediterranean naval scene had at least five crucial and immediate implications. First, it was achieved without any decisive sea battle. The Muslim naval might was pushed aside with little resistance. Second, a relatively safe sea link for the Christians between the shores of Europe and those of the Eastern Mediterranean made it possible for the Crusaders' conquest to last two hundred years; the Muslim navy and its great rival, the Byzantine, became of secondary importance in rapid succession. But the Muslim navy had no real successor (on the Ottoman navy see below), whereas the Byzantine navy was succeeded by a number of mighty Christian navies: those of the Frankish, mainly Italian, maritime states. The Crusaders' occupation of Muslim territory did come to an end, but this had little effect on the growing Christian naval preponderance. Fourth, Muslim naval might, especially after the Fatimids moved their capital from the Maghreb to Egypt in the second half of the tenth century, became increasingly centered in the Eastern half of the Mediterranean. By contrast, Western Europe had a growing number of powerful naval centers inside and outside that sea. Fifth, looking at the map of the Mediterranean in the 11th and 12th centuries one gets the very convincing impression that Europe, which started its emergence not long before, was being threatened by a formidable pincer of Muslim Mediterannean lands, with their great hinterlands and with Muslim footholds in the European continent. With the hindsight we have now we know that that threat was far less than it looked at the time. A number of tiny maritime states turned the scales on sea, and the Muslim withdrawal from Spain had already started.

The implications for the more distant future were far greater. As is so well known, the Western Europeans wanted to reach India and bypass the Muslim world by seeking alternative routes in the Southeast and the West. The westward search resulted in the discovery of America, and the Southeastern one resulted in the circumnavigation of the Cape of Good Hope. Thus were established the basic lines of the map of our globe. The Muslim adversary whom it was intended to bypass was the only one on earth who could offer any kind of resistance to that far-reaching Western European expansion. The futility of that resistance was quickly apparent.

In the groping southeastward, which was led by the Portuguese, a relatively small flotilla, thousands of miles from its home base, managed to do away with the Mamluk navy practically overnight, even though the latter had received considerable help from the Ottomans. Thus ended a nearly exclusive Muslim naval hegemony in those wide expanses which had lasted for nine hundred years, and the foundation was laid for centuries of European dominance in that immense area. Worthy of particular note is that in this short and decisive naval struggle between Islam and Christianity, the navies of India and China, if there were such, were conspicuous by their absence. Neither was their appearance noticeable afterwards, at least for a very long time.

As for the European expansion westward, which, in the long run, proved to be even more important than the one to the Southeast, the Muslims had no choice but to watch it from afar, perhaps without realizing its meaning and consequences. The Ottoman Empire, which at that time was nearing the peak of its power, and which possessed a relatively strong navy, was locked in the Mediterranean, the Black Sea, the Red Sea and the Persian Gulf (from which abortive incursions into the Indian Ocean were carried out).[11] The main importance of its navy was, in my view, that it formed an essential complement to the Ottoman land army, threatening the heart of Europe.

In our move from sea to land, we shall return briefly to the period of the Crusades. The Muslim recognition that they had no chance of wresting naval hegemony from the Franks in the foreseeable future is demonstrated by the systematic destruction of the Syro-Palestinian coast from Ashkelon to Alexandretta (and, to a much more limited extent, even the coast of Egypt), with particular stress on the Palestinian section of that coast, for obvious reasons. The initiator of that coastal destruction was none other than the venerated Saladin (in 1191). He was followed by the greatest Mamluk Sultans: Baybars I, Qalaun, and his son al-Ashraf Khalīl, the conqueror of Acre. This was not at all a "scorched earth" policy, the target of which is usually temporary, but a policy aimed at a long-term perpetuation of the destruction. Such a destruction of his own territory by its defender, has no parallel, and especially not in a region which played such an important role in the history of mankind. The scope, meaning, and implications of that destruction have not attracted the attention they deserve.

In closing our sea power review, it should be mentioned that the Franks seem to have had a reasonable chance of breaking the land power of Islam in the later Middle Ages, albeit indirectly (as a preliminary to a direct attack). The Franks were well aware of this opportunity. The indirect way was sea blockade, as part of a general economic boycott. By means of it the Muslims would have been deprived of raw materials (mainly metals and wood, which were also essential for the war machine), and above all, of Mamluks, many of whom had been brought over by sea, often on Frankish ships. Such plans were current mainly after the Crusades, but had earlier roots. They were never carried out systematically.

I shall briefly review the Muslim-Christian struggle on land from the period of the Crusades onward. During that period the importance of the Mamluk might was repeatedly revealed.

The Fatimids, who were the first Muslim empire based in Egypt to face the Crusaders (Egypt was the key of the whole struggle), were the least successful for a number of reasons, some of which are quite well known. Here I shall deal very briefly with one major reason, which is much less well known. The Fatimids could not build a proper Mamluk army because they were blocked by Sunnī enemy states controling the routes leading to the far away Mamluk homelands and, just as significantly, because they came from the Maghreb with an already well established hierarchy and armed forces, to which they owed a great deal. They were unable to overcome the resistance of all those veteran elements. The combination of those two factors forced them, rather too late, to found military schools for novices in which Mamluk principles were either ignored or only partly carried out. On such shaky foundations no real Mamluk army could be formed.

The Ayyubids, who started their career as commanders in a Mamluk dynasty (the Zangids), whose main army was a Mamluk one, also based their might on Mamluks. Their Kurdish military element was of secondary importance, in spite of the fact that the Ayyubids themselves were Kurds. Their major victories were achieved mainly by their Mamluks, and this fact became even more pronounced toward the end of their rule.

The justified conviction that whichever of the two rivals ruled Egypt would also be the master of Syria and Palestine was shared by Muslims and Crusaders. The last Frankish attempt to conquer Egypt (1248) was also the biggest. This attempt was made under the command of Louis IX (St. Louis). In the famous battle of al-Manṣūra, in Lower Egypt, the huge Frankish army was defeated by the Mamluk regiment of the Baḥriyya, which later founded the Mamluk Sultanate, and St. Louis was taken prisoner. During the whole history of Islam, only two first-ranking Christian kings were captured. The first was the Byzantine Emperor Romanus Diogenes in 1071 (the battle of Manzikert), and the second Louis IX. The armies of both were defeated by Mamluks.

When the Mamluks of the Mamluk Sultanate (1250–1517) came to power, they put an end to the Crusaders' rule on the one hand, and stopped the Mongol tide on the other. They were the first defenders in all of the Mongol attacks to check the Mongols (the battle of ʿAyn Jalūt, 1260). And what is even more important, they held them back in three much bigger battles in Northern Syria (although in one of them they were the losers).

Toward the middle of the thirteenth century, Islam's prospects looked very gloomy. In the West (Spain) the Muslims were on the defensive, losing ground to a determined Christian rival. In the center the Crusaders, still in possession of substantial parts of Syria, threatened Egypt with an imminent invasion of unprecedented scale. And in the East the Mongol tempest was advancing inexorably toward the heart of the Muslim world, leaving behind it destruction and slaughter of hitherto unknown dimensions; was within sight of the conquest of Iraq and the abolishment of the Caliphate; and had the undisguised intention of overrunning Syria and Egypt. The danger that an anti-Muslim coalition of the Franks and the Mongols would be formed became more concrete. Some serious attempts to create such a coalition were made. Under the circumstances of such an imminent and colossal danger one could not expect the threatened Muslims to think more calmly and adopt the longer view, namely, that those same Mongols would ultimately convert to Islam, in spite of the strong inclination of some of their rulers to convert to Christianity. It was even more difficult for them to think that way because the Mongols were not their next-door neighbors, with whom they were acquainted, but strangers from a faraway country who had descended on them like a bolt from the blue. They needed time and tranquility to see the other side of this invasion.

The immediate future thus looked extremely gloomy, and the fears of the contemporary Muslims that Islam was nearing its end, repeated so often in alarming terms in the sources, did not appear to be groundless. Casting a still gloomier pall was the recognition that no succor could be expected from the still unsubjugated lands of Islam: Arabia and the countries lying to the West of Egypt, up to and including Spain. This gloomy outlook was transformed by the Mamluks who, in the crucial area, removed both the Crusaders' and the Mongols' threat within a short space of time.

From this point on, the very existence of the Mamluk Sultanate was of the highest importance. It formed a barrier against the Franks, the like of which never existed before. The fact that the Crusades were not renewed was not only owing to the dissensions in the Western camp, but also, and perhaps to no smaller extent, owing to the existence of that barrier.

The Ottoman Empire, a Mamluk state as well, although of a special brand, went even much further. It extended Islam's boundaries into Europe, and after it started declining, it still formed, during a very long period, a defensive factor of the highest importance.

Thus, these two Mamluk great powers formed a strong wall against European penetration into Islam's heartland that lasted for centuries. Without them, or, more precisely, in the absence of the Mamluk system, Europe would have been sucked into a military vacuum in the Middle East (perhaps unintentionally). These two powers were undoubtedly the main cause for the fact that five hundred years separated the end of the Crusades in the last decade of the thirteenth century and the French occupation of Egypt toward the end of the eighteenth. Between these two dates, far-reaching changes took place in Europe, and the aims of modern imperialism diverged fundamentally from those of the Crusades.

It is obvious that the Mamluk socio-military system could not withstand the growing European technological superiority indefinitely . Even the Ottoman Empire, which, generally speaking, was much more ready to absorb technological and other innovations, could not do so. Its industrial basis was weak from the outset, and the more the links between industry and arms production strengthened, the more remote were the chances of the Ottoman Empire at garnering great military achievements.

A brief comparison between the conquest of Egypt and Syria from Anatolia by the Ottomans at the beginning of the sixteenth century and the conquest of Syria and considerable parts of Anatolia from Egypt by Muḥammad ʿAlī in the first half of the nineteenth (an interval of more than three hundred years) should be useful at this point.

As already stated, the map of the world was transformed in the transition period between the fifteenth and the sixteenth centuries. This transformation resulted not only from the Western European expansion, which took place mainly outside the boundaries of the Abode of Islam; but also from the shift of the center of gravity within these boundaries. That its center of gravity moved from Cairo to Istanbul, following the huge Ottoman onslaught to the East and to the South, that was carried out inside Muslim territory. Simultaneously with that thrust, a strongly motivated Shiʿite empire (the Safawids) rose in Iran, which created a new situation in the struggle between the Sunna and the Shiʿa. It is true that at that period the Muslims could do practically nothing to stop or hinder European expansion beyond the seas, but at the same time the Europeans' ability to intervene in events in the major Muslim countries was very limited indeed. Furthermore, the empire, which had the upper hand in the internal Muslim struggle, then threatened the heart of Europe quite seriously (an outlet for European intervention was the common interest of the Safawids and the Central European Christians to curb the Ottomans).

Under Muḥammad ʿAlī a totally different picture emerged. In order to realize his dreams of expansion this ruler justly decided to wipe out the old Muslim structure of the army and build a totally new army on a European model. He was the first ruler to carry out such a revolutionary measure in the whole of Africa and Asia, including the Pacific Islands. It opened the widest gate to westernization. Muḥammad ʿAlī's first decisive step (1811) within the execution of his plan was to finish off the Mamluk cavalrymen, together with their whole socio-military system. This step was complemented by settling the Bedouins (another cavalry element) on the soil. After that came the gradual buildup of his land army and navy under the guidance and supervision of French experts. After some gropings and unsuccessful attempts, the Egyptian fellah, an infantryman, was chosen to form the backbone of the land army (up to and not including the officers' ranks). The great advantage of the Egyptian fellah, beyond his proverbial power of endurance, was that he lacked any military tradition, and it was therefore easy to mold him in accordance with new needs.

Muḥammad ʿAlī's military success, which started long before the completion of his plan, surpassed all expectations. Within about twenty years, Egypt made conquests unlike any before or since: most of the Arabian Peninsula (against a strongly motivated adversary, the Wahhabis); the Sudan; and, above all, Syria, followed by a very deep advance in Anatolia. Between the conquest of the Sudan and the invasion of Syria, the Egyptian navy and army formed the main factor in the fight against the Greek rebels. That astounding achievement was made possible because of Muḥammad ʿAlī's vision and leadership; because that ruler finished off the antiquated Mamluks fifteen years before the Ottoman Sultan did the same to the antiquated janissaries (1826); and because of the centralized character of Egypt and its relatively small size, which made it easier to transform the army completely.

But at this very point the Egyptian ruler's basic weakness also came to the fore. When his victorious army was already in the heart of Anatolia and threatened Istanbul, he was forced to yield to the European Powers' dictate and surrender most of the conquered Anatolian territories. After some years he was forced to evacuate Syria as a result of another European dictate, accompanied by little fighting. But for the conflicting interests of those powers, his occupation of Syria would have ended considerably earlier. A forerunner of this kind of development was the October 1827 defeat in Navarino of the Turkish-Egyptian fleet by a combined British, French, and Russian naval force, which contributed so much to the establishment of the independence of Greece. On top of that the great dream of Muḥammad ʿAlī came to naught because it was out of all proportion to the limited resources of Egypt (on Western economic superiority to that of Islam, see below).

Whatever the case may be, Muḥammad ʿAlī's westernization of his army was a precursor of the future. Today, and even much earlier than today, all the non-European navies and armies have little connection to their historical military tradition. Excluding certain frills, and a deeply rooted feeling of belonging to a particular civilization or nation with its rich and glorious heritage, all these are armies molded on the Western model. This westernization is even more evident in modern non-

European air forces and missile and atomic bomb units, with far-reaching repercussions far beyond the military domain. In many other domains, not necessarily connected with the army, one encounters the same or a similar situation.

The Cause of Western Superiority—A Tentative Explanation

The above exposé raises the obvious question: Why? What are the reasons for the immense gap between Western civilization and all the other ones, and for the enormous impact of that civilization on all those others? Before trying to answer this vital question, I would like to make two observations.

A. Putting one's finger on a certain phenomenon and drawing a picture of it is one thing; offering an explanation of its origins is quite another. This is true of all scholarly disciplines, including the sciences. Establishing a certain fact and explaining it are not necessarily simultaneous. My main claim here is that the lagging of Islam behind the West started as far back as the eleventh century, if not earlier. Thus, this lag began (in reverse chronological order) before the French Revolution, before the Industrial Revolution, before the Reformation, before the Renaissance, before the invention of printing, and even more than two hundred years before the introduction of firearms in Europe in the first half of the fourteenth century; furthermore, also before what is now called the European renaissance of the twelfth century. All these major events were the culmination of long processes, which we may or may not unveil. The important thing is that these processes alone, even before reaching their culmination, were sufficient to give Western Europe its great push forward. Therefore, the explanation should be from this angle, from this vantage point.

B. Military preponderance as a reliable yardstick for technological and other superiority certainly has its drawbacks. Yet its advantages far outweigh them, for two reasons. a) This preponderance in itself is a result of a whole set of factors belonging to many domains, which are not confined to the purely military. b) Its great achievements, which make other civilizations adopt it, pave a very wide way for other elements of Western civilization, including those which are absolutely non-military, to penetrate into those other civilizations.

Returning to the explanation, I would like to emphasize that it is a partial and tentative attempt, made by a non-expert of European history. In my view, the relative flexibility of Christian monotheism was one of the decisive factors. Similarly important was the development in Christianity of two separate, and often competing, entities of Church and State. This separatedness was, to no small extent, the result of the history of Christianity. After centuries of persecutions, following its inception, it was adopted by a great ruler as the official religion of his state. Until then, however, it had to fend for itself under very difficult and dangerous conditions. In order to survive and spread it had to build its institutions and its hierarchy. The lay ruler received a quite well organized clergy, which he had to accept more or less as it was. This fact facilitated, to a great extent, the gradual separation of the Church and State, and thus ultimately brought about the secular Modern State. In addition, in Europe, because of the special conditions created after the demise of the Roman empire, the feudal system came into being, and with it the antagonism and competition of the ruler who lived in town and his noblemen, living in the country in their feudal fiefs. On top of all that, the European free cities formed an important separate entity to be reckoned with. This is a formidable set of factors, with the first one at its heart. The existence of several centers of power allowed the creation of different and changing combinations between them, in which forbidden, unaccepted or unconventional thinking could live, or at least survive (perhaps not always, but quite often).

In Islam these factors did not exist. The period of its persecution was very short and ended early in the lifetime of its founder, the prophet Muḥammad. The headship of the Muslim religion and the Muslim state were inseparably combined and embodied in his person. His successors, the Caliphs, inherited all his powers, with the significant exception of prophecy. When the Muslim Arabs burst out of their peninsula, they conquered with relative ease well-developed urban areas, which suffered only little damage as a result of conquest. From the beginning, practically everything was concentrated in the town, including the new military towns built by the conquerors. The Muslim dominant society (the governing, the military and the religious), was mainly urban. The military fiefs were, indeed, in the country but most of their lords were absentees, dwelling in town. All these bodies were inseparably interlocked; all that with the absence in Islam of Church and State from the very outset.

It seems to me that the relative flexibility of Christian monotheism, and the European developments mentioned above, together with the classical heritage (see below), were some of the most important factors responsible for the great jump forward of Western civilization as compared with the other civilizations. As I have already tried to show, the first great manifestations of that jump forward came at least as early as the eleventh century.

We shall start with the monotheistic civilizations.

The absolute monotheism of Judaism and Islam did not allow a development similar to that which took place in Christianity. I shall bring two examples to this effect, but first I find it necessary to make the following qualification. Within the context of our subject it is rather unfair to put Judaism on the same footing as Islam and Christianity. Had the Jews not been exiled from their country, and had they during their stay cultivated a desire to convert the whole world to Judaism, or at least to put it under Jewish sway, and had they been as successful as these two other monotheistic religions in realizing that desire, then and only then it would be justified to include Judaism in the comparison. On the other hand, it would be rather improper to ignore the mother of monotheism completely in our context.

And now to the two examples.

It seems to me that there was little chance for the Jewish Yeshiva or the Muslim Madrasa to develop into a university by exclusively internal processes, as the universities did develop in Europe from the higher institutions of learning, where the study of religion occupied a central place. It also seems to me that neither in Judaism nor in Islam could one arrive at the conclusion that our earth is not the center of the Universe, but just a small planet orbiting the Sun. Furthermore, it is even less likely that that conclusion, with all that it signifies and implies, would become a central issue, and finally would be accepted.

In Christianity there was some elbow room, albeit very narrow, which made those developments possible, after a long and bitter struggle.

There was room for challenge and response, within the ramifications of a stubborn antagonism. No such elbow room existed in the two other monotheistic religions. In Judaism, developments of this kind could take place only when the barriers between the European Jews and the Christian society within which they lived were removed to some extent. In Islam, this occurred only after a long period of military inferiority vis-à-vis the West.

It is certainly true, and widely known, that a substantial part of the classical heritage reached the West through Islam and in Arabic translation. The enlightened world owes it a great debt for that. But the question arises: up to what point and in what direction could that heritage develop within Islam? I do not think it could develop there in the way it developed within Christianity. It is true that Muslim philosophy and cosmology, and sciences in general, were on the wane when the great breakthroughs in the West took place. But let us suppose, for argument's sake, that they reached their peak at that time. Even in such a hypothetical situation, they would have faced limits beyond which they would not have been able to go. In my opinion it is absolutely impossible that Muslim philosophers and cosmographers would have ever tried seriously to change our view of the Universe, in the way their counterparts did in Europe, to say nothing about succeeding in such an attempt.

Developments in the sciences are closely connected with those of the humanities. The scholarly tools we use and the methods that guide us in this vast domain are mainly an outgrowth of Western Civilization. This is true of classical philology and not less true of the study of the Holy Scriptures, both of which profoundly effect practically every humanistic branch. Once again, neither in Judaism nor in Islam could those tools and that method come into being from within.

Concerning the impact of the classical and postclassical period on Christianity, as compared with its impact on Islam, it should be borne in mind that the first, which is about six hundred years older than the second, grew up and spread during that long period in the Hellenistic world, and absorbed from it directly much of its culture and values (besides writings which did not reach it through the Muslim channel). This kind of absorption was bound to affect all of Christian society to some degree from top to bottom. This raises, of course, the question of how much classical and postclassical culture influenced Muslim society beyond the layer of its intellectuals.

The fact that the ruler, the ruling class, and the religious leadership in Islam were town dwellers and were intertwined might raise the argument that the ruler, who was at the top of that pyramid, could impose his will to carry out changes leading to developments similar to those which took place in Christian Europe. Such developments were highly unlikely, however. First of all, the other factors, existing in Christianity, and enumerated above, were lacking in Islam. Second, the ruler and his whole hierarchy did not feel the need for changes of this kind. They had no doubt as to the absolute superiority of their religion and of the values, way of life, and way of thinking to which it gave birth. This was true of practically all the rulers, and at least as true of the rulers of slave origin, who were taught that they were led not only from anonymity to fame and from poverty to richness, but even more so from the depths of infidel darkness (*ẓulumāt*) to the heights of the veritable Muslim light (*huda*). Since Islam was victorious for many years, and on a par with Christianity for yet another long period, the Muslim rulers had little incentive to change. In the military domain they were, generally speaking, more inclined to absorb external influences even before Islam's might began its decline. That inclination grew as that might weakened. The conviction of these rulers about Islam's superiority, however, lasted much longer, and more often than not never died out. But the cruel reality of repeated and heavier defeats, which continued for centuries, with no prospects of change for the better, forced them, one after the other, to carry out comprehensive reforms of their armies. These reforms created the main breach through which Westernization entered the lands of Islam with different degrees of success.

Russia is an instructive instance of how much more easily a Christian country could accept and absorb the achievements of Western civilization than countries belonging to non-Christian civilizations even when its starting point was very low. This Christian Orthodox country began its Westernization under Peter the Great at the turn of the eighteenth century, about a hundred years before Muḥammad ʿAlī. Relatively quickly it became one of the mightiest European military powers, which threatened, inter alia, the very existence of the Ottoman Empire, and which advanced eastwards up to the shores of the Pacific Ocean, thus completing the earlier Christian expansion over the globe. In spite of its very distinct character, its culture, in the widest sense of the word, merges, on the whole, far more naturally with that of the West than that of any other civilization.

A factor of the first magnitude in weakening the hold of the central government in Islam beyond the urban centers were the nomads, or, in a wider sense, the peoples belonging to tribal societies. Before the advent of Islam there were two big tribal bodies in the whole area stretching from the Atlantic Ocean to the mountains of Kurdistan, with the obvious exception of Arabia and its immediate vicinity: the Berbers in the West, and the Kurds in the Northeast. The immense gap between the two was filled in two stages: by the Arab tribes from the beginning of the spread of Islam and by the Turkish tribes from the beginning of the eleventh century onward. Thus, almost all the countryside of that vast area was covered by tribesmen, with their own allegiances, internal and external relations, and struggles; command of the many major routes, and revolts against as well as cooperation with the rulers that be. This subject deserves a comprehensive and detailed study in an all-Muslim context. Here I shall confine myself to two matters. One is that cavalry was the backbone of the armies of at least the Arab and the Turkish tribesmen, like that of the Mamluks (themselves coming from the tribal, mainly Turkish societies) and that of the Mongol Islamized latecomers. Horsemanship typified the bulk of the Muslim privileged armies far beyond the Mamluk institution (with the important exception of the janissary infantry). This might have been helpful to Islam for a considerable period, but in the long run it made it much more difficult to modernize Islam's military might. The second matter is that tribal and nomadic systems did have some positive economic aspects, but on balance their negative impact on the economy was far greater. Relatively small armies, like that of the Mamluks, could be successful within a rather weak economy. This became more difficult with the development of modern warfare, which entailed the mobilization of all the economic and other resources. Whereas in Islam nomadism and tribalism remained an important factor almost up to the present day,[12] in Europe they played a marginal and diminishing role, if any, and they did not weigh heavily on the European economy. Cavalry-mindedness did persist even in Europe well into the twentieth century, but it was not as deeply rooted or as widespread as in Islam. These were just two of its numerous advantages vis-à-vis its Islamic counterpart.

It would appear that the texture created in Western Civilization managed to absorb and digest the innovations that came from the outside, blending them with its own, in a way that no other civilization, including those which gave them birth, could do. This explains perhaps the tremendous and unprecedented impact on land, on sea, in the air and beyond which Western Civilization has been making on all the other civilizations, overshadowing so thoroughly the impact in the opposite direction, which is by no means negligible.[13]

After all that had been said, one can not but raise the obvious question: Where does all this lead? This great and unparalleled leap forward, which is accelerated almost from day to day, exposes the human race to the most real threat of self-annihilation. Such a threat had never been known before, and not only because of the atomic bomb. One cannot but hope and pray that the destructive instinct of the human being will be subdued by the instinct for self-preservation.

Notes

Professor Ayalon did not have the opportunity to review proofs for his contribution to this volume. We are privileged, however, to present the above essay by the learned scholar who can justly be described as the founder of Mamluk studies.

1. The region enveloped by the Oxus and the Yaxartes (or the Amu Darya and the Syr Darya), both flowing into the Aral Sea.
2. Not only blacks served as infantrymen in Islam. Infantry was particularly important where the maneuverability of cavalry was limited, such as in mountainous areas, as well as in sieges. The attitude to blacks outside the military is a different story.
3. The common frontier between Islam and China is not discussed here because the extent of the Turkish layer separating them is not clear, and because no human influx of any significance or durability entered Islam from China, especially during the early centuries of its existence.

4. The Turkish Mamluks and the Turks took a decisive part in the struggle between the Sunna and the Shiʿa. Within the framework of the thesis presented here this subject deserves special scrutiny.

5. The same goes, of course, for Muslim rulers or other Muslims entering the lands of Christianity.

6. Another characteristic feature common to the three elements was that they all were horsemen. On this subject see also below.

7. "The Great Yāsa of Chingiz Khān: A Re-examination," *Studia Islamica* 36 (1972), pp. 113–58.

8. I have pointed out the Mamluk character of the main body of the Seljuk army on several occasions. However, it deserves special treatment. Its importance in the study of the Mamluk phenomenon lies in the fact that it forms the major connecting link between the Mamluk army of the ʿAbbasids and those of later Muslim rulers.

9. There were, of course, mutual linguistic influences in the first front, but they were minor in comparison with those of the East.

10. *Ḥawādith al-Duhūr* (ed. Popper), p. 290, ll. 13–17.

11. The incursions of the corsairs outside the Mediterranean were also temporary. Furthermore, the share of the Christian European converts in those incursions and in building the ships for carrying them out was very great indeed.

12. Needless to say, the Bedouins' share in weakening the hold of the central government on the countryside, and the fact that their Islamic awareness was not the strongest, contributed little to openness in Islam.

13. The impressive emergence of the Far East is still too young to be discussed in a historical perspective. For the time being it is competing successfully with the West mainly by means of the tools created by that West.

CPSIA information can be obtained
at www.ICGtesting.com
Printed in the USA
LVOW08s1710180118
563129LV00004B/248/P